CARA

Growing With a Retarded Child

Martha Moraghan Jablow

TEMPLE UNIVERSITY PRESS · PHILADELPHIA

Temple University Press

© 1982 by Temple University. All rights reserved

Published 1982

Printed in the United States of America

Library of Congress Cataloging in Publication Data

Jablow, Martha Moraghan.
Cara, growing with a retarded child.

Bibliography: p.
Includes index.
1. Mentally handicapped children—Family
relationships.   2. Child development.
3. Mentally handicapped children—Education.
4. Down's syndrome.   I. Title.
HV891.J3   362.3′092′4   82-3283
ISBN 0-87722-255-X   AACR2
ISBN 0-87722-269-X (pbk.)

Although retarded children may be
the victims of fate,
they will not be the victims
of our neglect.

John Fitzgerald Kennedy
1963

To Ada Welton Pratt,

Cara's great-grandmother,

who always called her

"dear, sweet little Cara."

CONTENTS

ILLUSTRATIONS

PREFACE

Eight years ago I was happily wallpapering a nursery for our first child, expected in a month. The wallpaper was a colorful print of the alphabet—a red "A" next to a picture of an apple, a "B" next to a blue butterfly . . . I finished the paper and was satisfied. Its brightness matched my mood.

A month later Cara was born. We soon learned that she has Down's syndrome, the most common form of mental retardation. Soon after this news, my husband Paul walked into Cara's room and stared at the wallpaper.

"I wonder if she'll ever be able to read those letters," he said sadly.

At Cara's birth, we knew little about mental retardation and even less about Down's syndrome. In the past eight years, we have learned a great deal. Cara has been our greatest teacher.

She can indeed read those letters. She knew the alphabet when she was two-and-a-half. Before she was five, she could read scores of three- and four-letter words. Today Cara is reading and writing with her first-grade classmates. She continually astounds us with her outpouring of language and love.

Cara is one of six million retarded persons in the United States. One in 1,000 babies is born with Down's syndrome, which comes to about 33,000 born in the United States during the past decade.

Cara is unique among these thousands. She was one of the first infants in the country to enroll in an intense training program for babies with developmental delays. Such programs, called infant stimulation or early intervention programs, are designed to give slow babies a head start on such basics as sitting alone, crawling, feeding themselves, walking and talking. Children in these programs have various forms of developmental delays such as Down's syndrome, cerebral palsy, brain damage, or microcephaly, or they may have an undiagnosed delay which may be caused by nutritional or emotional deprivation.

Most babies, we assume, learn to crawl and walk and talk naturally. But for a child born with a mental or physical handicap, these accomplishments come later and with much more effort.

Cara began school at one month of age. When children like Cara can spend four mornings a week with skilled, loving teachers who guide them through exercises and activities to strengthen their muscles and minds, they can reach milestones earlier than if they were left alone to "do it when they are ready," as some old-fashioned professionals would say.

Our experience with Cara has convinced us that she is accomplishing far more than other handicapped children who have not had the good fortune of attending an early intervention program. We are just as thoroughly convinced that, because she got off to a running start from one month of age, she will be a far more independent and productive adult than if she had been left alone at home or in an institution.

Cara has already shattered most of the milestones usually associated with Down's syndrome. Current literature on Down's syndrome says, for instance, that a Down's child "will usually sit without support about 13 months of age." Cara sat alone at eight months. Or, "independent walking usually takes place on an average of 27 months but may be delayed in some cases to four years." Cara walked independently at eighteen months. Or, "speech is delayed so that *some* speech is generally present by the age of four years." Cara had a vocabulary of 75 to 100 words at two-and-a-half, and by age four was speaking in complete five- and six-word sentences. I would say that this is more than "some speech."

Her language is so close to normal that at age three years, seven months, she tested at a three-year, five-month level on a speech and language test. That was a Catch-22 situation—she was "so normal," as the speech therapist said, that she could not qualify for a speech therapy program for delayed preschoolers.

Three months before she turned five, Cara began to read by phonetically sounding out almost any three- or four-letter word.

I mention these facts not to boast about Cara, though I am immensely proud of her, but to emphasize that the myths about the abilities of the retarded are crumbling as more and more retarded children are exposed to early intervention programs.

I tell Cara's story not only out of a mother's love, but also because there are many parents and professionals who can learn from her experiences. The activities described in this book can be applied to any child with a developmental delay, depending on his or her particular need at a given point of development. Whether children have brain damage or Down's syndrome, they must learn to bear weight on their feet before they can walk. And identical exercises can be used for each child.

These activities can be used for normal children as well. I have learned a great deal about child development from Cara's program that I have applied to David, her younger, normal brother.

Dr. Burton L. White, who has spent a career researching child development, wrote in his book, *The First Three Years of Life*, "Those first years are far more important than we had previously thought. In their simple everyday activities, infants and toddlers form the foundation of *all* later development."

I believe Dr. White. And I'll go further: for the child who begins life behind the rest of the pack, those first years are even more crucial. If those years are full of enriching, stimulating experiences that help the child to explore the world, master physical skills and become as self-sufficient and self-confident as possible, then that child will be more of a joy to his or her family and less of a burden to society as an adult.

As a society, we should begin immediately to pour our resources into helping delayed children during their first five years rather than waiting until they are eighteen, when they are taught to sort silverware or weave baskets in a sheltered workshop.

CARA

ONE

"I Wonder if She'll Ever Be Able to

Read Those Letters"

Damn slippers. How dumb to bring these heel-torturers to the hospital. What unwritten code requires presentable slippers on the maternity floor? Is it part of some ritual: when your due date is near, dear, pack your suitcase early and include pretty slippers?

These gold brocade things with their fake silk lining weren't my style anyway. They looked like they came out of "The King and I" wardrobe closet. Why hadn't I brought my comfortable, grubby old slippers?

My thoughts rambled this trivial route as I walked down the hall, on the balls of my feet, to the nursery. Within minutes my mundane thoughts about stiff slippers would be deluged by serious thoughts, as if a twenty-foot wave had crashed down on tiny beach pebbles.

I had left Cara in the nursery while I showered. Except for my heels, I was happy. Today was Saturday, the day we would take three-day-old Cara Kathleen Jablow home. Paul would come in an hour to pick us up. His mother had arrived at the house on Thursday. My parents were on their way.

Cara's birth had been easy. Our Lamaze prepared childbirth classes stood us well as Paul coached my labor by timing contractions, rubbing my aching back, and giving me styrofoam cups of crushed ice to quench my thirst.

We entered Booth Maternity Center in Philadelphia about 9:00 A.M. on

February 27, 1974. Cara was born at 1:05 P.M. A breeze of a delivery, I thought, though personally I had none other to compare it to. The Lamaze classes had taught me what to expect and how to breathe during labor. I had no sedation or pain-killer, and no episiotomy and, therefore, no stitches from which to recover. Fernand Lamaze, the French physician who pioneered prepared childbirth techniques, would have been proud of me. Cara's birth left me exhilarated.

Cara was tiny and sweet. Only five pounds, nine ounces. Nineteen-and-a-half inches long. We had not expected a linebacker of a baby. My obstetrician, Dr. John Franklin, had predicted during one of my last prenatal checkups that the baby might be about six pounds.

"Go out and have a milkshake," he said, "You can afford it." I went directly to a Howard Johnson's.

Cara's small birth weight came as no surprise because neither Paul nor I are very large people. We didn't care if she was tiny. She was beautiful.

Like all newborns, Cara was given the Apgar test immediately after birth. Named for its originator, Dr. Virginia Apgar, the procedure checks heart rate, respiration, muscle tone, reflexes and skin color. It is given one minute after birth and again after five minutes. The highest possible score is ten. Cara scored nine on the first round (losing a point for less than rosy skin color) and ten on the second round when she gained a healthy pink. They were excellent scores, as I boasted to my mother on the phone a half hour later.

Booth Maternity Center has a rooming-in policy which encourages mothers to keep their newborns at their bedsides as much as they wish. It is a warm, natural way for mother and baby to get acquainted. Cara had been constantly with me over her first three days in room 235. Fathers were also allowed to visit in the mother's room from 9:00 A.M. to 9:00 P.M. for as long and as often as they wished. Cara had already spent much time in her father's green-hospital-robed arms. We grew to know Cara in these first three days as we stroked her smooth skin, held her little body and played with her tiny fingers and toes. She slept much of the time and rarely fussed.

The only thing that disturbed me was her disinterest in nursing. Several of the nurses and midwives suggested stroking her chin and cheeks to stimulate sucking. One Scottish nurse suggested holding her in the curious "football carry" position while nursing, with Cara's fanny tucked on my hip and her legs dangling behind me. It appeared backward to an onlooker but it occasionally worked—I have no idea why. For the most part though, she did not seem interested in nursing. By contrast, the big bruiser in the next bed was exhausting his mother with his constant demands to be fed.

But with the nurses reassuring me that she would catch on, Cara's lack of interest in nursing did not seem a matter of serious concern. So my thoughts focused on the trivial—my hurting heels—as I walked down the hall toward the nursery.

I had wheeled Cara in her little bassinet cart to the nursery so I could shower. I was walking down the hall to toss my old hospital gown in the laundry chute and to retrieve Cara when I noticed Dr. Allen Chandler, the staff pediatrician, coming toward me. I greeted him with a smile and a hello. He returned the hello but not the smile.

"How are you?" he asked, taking my left hand and turning to walk back toward the nursery with me.

"Fine, just great," I answered. Strange behavior, I thought. He had not struck me as the hand-holding type.

"I want to talk with you," he said. Apprehension clouded his brown eyes in a look that I was to see several times over the coming weeks. I tensed slightly. At that moment I knew him only from the brief encounter the day before when he came into room 235 to examine Cara and the bruiser in the next bed. When he came over to our side of the room, washed in bright February sunlight, he had looked Cara over in a rather cursory way. I thought little of it because I knew he had given her a thorough examination the previous day in the nursery. I did not know that he was holding serious fears close to his vest.

He still held my hand as we rounded the corner by the nurses' station and entered the nursery.

"There are a few things about Cara that concern me," he began. "You notice her skin color, how it's yellowish? Well, that's a touch of jaundice. It's not uncommon in new babies. But I'd like to keep her here a day or so more. We will put her under a bilirubin lamp until it improves." He went on to explain that a newborn's liver often is not mature enough to take care of the old red blood cells which the body must cast off. The bilirubin lamp speeds this process as the young liver matures.

"I thought you seemed pretty somber yesterday when you examined her," I said.

"No, I wasn't my usual jovial self," he replied. "There is something else. How old are you and your husband?"

"I'm twenty-nine and Paul is thirty-three. Why?"

"Well, have you ever heard of a chromosomal abnormality called Down's syndrome where there is an extra chromosome in each cell of the body?"

"I don't know. The only chromosome abnormality I can think of is that Richard Speck thing—the guy who killed those Chicago nurses years ago. Didn't they think he was unusually violent because he had an extra "Y" chromosome?"

"No, no. Not that." Dr. Chandler seemed to fumble for the right words to express this problem as much as I fumbled to grasp it.

"The things that concern me about Cara are her floppy muscle tone and the slant of her eyes," he continued. "You see, this is firm muscle tone," he said, grasping both my hands with his and giving a mild pull. "Now you see how Cara's is floppy?" He wrapped her tiny fingers around one of my fingers. There was little grasp or pull.

"Yes, but isn't that the way all new babies are?" I asked.

"No. There should be more resilience. And look at her eyes. Do you see how they are slanted slightly upward in an oriental way, or almond-shaped?"

"No, I can't tell with her eyes closed." I was already beginning to deny what I could not completely comprehend. This conversation is a muddle, I thought. He's telling me something very serious but I don't understand it. And I, the old reporter, can't come up with the right questions.

"Well, what does this mean?" I managed to ask.

"Now, I want you to understand that I'm not making a positive diagnosis on Cara. The eyes and the muscle tone are just two signs of Down's syndrome. There are other signs which she doesn't have, like a heart murmur or a single crease in the palm of her hand. I listened very carefully for a heart murmur and she doesn't have one."

"Well, if she does have this Down's syndrome, what happens in the long run?" My questions were gropingly inadequate.

"Most of these children are very happy, loving children who fit right into family life at home. But in some cases, families think about institutionalization," he said.

That was the first moment of truth. Dr. Chandler in these few minutes had not used the words "mental retardation," but the word "institutionalization" drove that message home. I could say nothing. I felt suddenly warm. My palms sweated.

"I'd like to talk with your husband, too," Dr. Chandler said.

"Well, he's coming about eleven to take us home, or he thinks he's going to take us home."

"I'll be in my other office then, in West Philadelphia. Where do you live?"

"In Mount Airy."

"So do I. I'll call your husband so we can see about getting together to talk some more," he said. Dr. Chandler seemed rushed, as if he wanted more than anything in the world to be out of that nursery. I knew just how he felt. He left and I stood looking down at Cara, that sweet, sleeping infant who looked so totally at peace. How could anything possibly be wrong with her?

My heels were numb to any pain as I walked back to room 235. My mind was equally numb. I called Paul.

"The pediatrician thinks Cara should stay here a few more days because she has jaundice. Come out here soon anyway. I think I may check out and come back to nurse her several times a day until she can come home. The doctor's a little concerned about her, but don't tell your mother that. He thinks she may have something called Down's syndrome. I'll tell you more about it when you come. Just tell your mother that Cara won't be coming home today."

Whatever went through my mind in that hour before Paul arrived is now a blur. I think I just tuned out reality and wished I were alone. I needed to sort out this confusion.

I remember physical details of that day more clearly than emotions. I remember, for instance, that Paul walked in wearing a maroon plaid shirt and maroon corduroy slacks. I remember that the curtain was drawn between my bed and the woman's on the other side of the room. I was grateful for the privacy.

I relayed what Dr. Chandler said as precisely as I could. Paul wasn't concerned about the jaundice because he remembered, as I had forgotten, that jaundice is common and not too serious in newborns. He did not know what Down's syndrome was.

Paul hadn't been in the hospital room more than five minutes when the phone rang. Paul sprang for it. It was Dr. Chandler. As I listened to Paul's end of the conversation, I realized that the doctor was being much more specific with Paul than he had been with me. Was it the man-to-man angle or the distance of a phone wire that made the difference?

"But what does that mean? How sure are you? What makes you suspect that?" Paul pressed him. Paul had been a newspaper reporter for ten years and knew how to use his interviewing skills to pry out as much information as possible.

Dr. Chandler was trying to provide information as gently as he could. He talked about chromosomes and genes. Paul remembers thinking, though not saying, "Come on, Doctor, cut the bull and get to the point."

Dr. Chandler went as far as saying, were he a betting man, he would wager that Cara's chances of having Down's syndrome might be 30 or 40 percent. But we wanted to know for certain. Dr. Chandler said he would arrange for chromosome tests which would confirm or deny his suspicions.

When Paul hung up the phone, he knew what Down's syndrome was. "It's mongolism. Mental retardation." The reporter minced no words.

"But he's not sure, Paul. He said he's not sure," I insisted.

I often come close to being a Pollyanna. Paul never does. He paces and rubs his hands together when he's worried. Hit with this news—the most weighty of his life—he did not react with his usual, outward nervous expressions. Tension tightened his face, but that was the only sign. We talked quietly about what Dr. Chandler had said. I was aware of the other new mother on the opposite side of the curtain.

Three years later, after we had grown to know Dr. Chandler better as our family pediatrician, he discussed more openly his feelings about diagnosing Cara.

"I was fairly positive she had Down's syndrome. But you don't go in and throw wet rags on the parents. That has happened. Some women have been told right on the delivery table, 'Mrs. So-and-So, your baby is retarded and may not live to leave this hospital.' The analogy would be, 'Mrs. Jablow, you have cancer.' The doctor discusses symptoms, the situation, over a period of time, letting it sink in. Then you know you have cancer without having been told outright. While you don't throw wet rags, you can't toss out false balloons of hope either. It's your child and you have every right to know the facts. We have no right to keep them from you. But the doctor has to let the parents know the positives, too. And that's why I told you that Down's syndrome children are loving and affectionate and fit in easily with family life."

Dr. Chandler was thirty-eight. He had seen only eight or ten newborns with Down's syndrome in his career. He was directly responsible for the care of only about half of those. His job of telling us his suspicions about Cara was awkward because we were strangers to him. He knew only our ages, where we lived, and that Paul was a reporter. He had to rely on his intuition about how to tell us.

"I read Paul as confused but wanting to know the facts. I read you as wanting the facts, too, but more slowly," he later told me.

On the phone with Paul, Dr. Chandler had used the word "mongolism." Now we both knew the name of the game. My mind flashed back fifteen years. My eighth-grade teacher had a mongoloid son. We often saw him at church with his parents and two big Marine Corps brothers. In contrast to his brothers, Patrick was short, a bit chubby, and wore a dull gaze. Patrick had always seemed a part of his family; he went everywhere with them. His mother was one of the best teachers I had ever had and my respect and affection for her translated into sympathetic acceptance of Patrick.

For Paul the term "mongolism" triggered the story of Jimmy Erskine, the son of former Brooklyn Dodger pitcher Carl Erskine. About a year before Cara's birth, Paul had read Roger Kahn's *The Boys of Summer*, a where-are-they-now tale of the 1950s Dodgers. In Chapter Five, Kahn visits the Erskine family in Anderson, Indiana, where Carl Erskine takes his nine-year-old mongoloid son swimming at the YMCA.

From those two flashbacks our knowledge of Down's syndrome began to grow. They were positive images from which to begin because both Patrick and Jimmy lived with their families and gave them much joy.

What to do next? While I had enjoyed my stay at Booth Maternity Center—having Cara next to me, the pampering by nurses who brought 9:00 P.M. snacks of ice cream and homemade cookies, and two full days of rest—I was suddenly anxious to escape. Today was the day to take Cara home, I had thought. The idea stuck in my mind but now I couldn't take her home. If she were to be sunbathing under the bilirubin lamp in the nursery all day and night, what good was I staying in a hospital bed I no longer needed? I decided to go home and return several times a day to nurse her—or to try to nurse her. She still showed little interest in mother's milk. The nursery nurses tried to interest her in bottles of milk or water but she seemed equally bored with them.

I now look back with some amusement on the way life's little details often orbit around the big events. In the crazy last hour in the hospital, with Paul's mind and mine whirring with troubling thoughts, questions and fears, I somehow remembered that I was about to miss a deadline. I had been doing some part-time reporting for *The New York Times*. A memo had been due in New York that day. I had completed most of the interviewing and writing before I entered the hospital. I had thrown the memo into my suitcase and taken it along to Booth with the notion that I might polish it off there. I never added a word. But in the last rush out of the hospital, I remembered it and scrawled a note across the top explaining that Cara's birth had interrupted my reporting. My handwriting was so shaky that I wondered if Jerry Flint, the editor, would be able to read it.

Jerry didn't hear of Cara's having Down's syndrome until a few months later. But when he received my note, he was so amused that he wrote a little story about it for "Times Talk," the house organ. Accompanying the story was a cartoon of me reclining in bed with a typewriter perched on top of my extremely pregnant belly. Eight months later Cara's picture ran with a story I wrote for *The Times* about an educational program for retarded babies, a story written at Jerry's suggestion.

Paul and I took one last look at Cara sleeping under the bilirubin lamp. Her little legs were pulled up under her stomach. She was a naked pink ball curled up on the white bassinet sheet. She wore only a white band of terry cloth around her head to protect her eyes from the lamp. We were tense, holding in all emotion.

It was a drizzling gray noon as we walked across the Booth parking lot to the yellow Volkswagen which should have been taking Cara for her first ride. Once inside the car, Paul couldn't put the key in the ignition. We held onto each other and cried silently for several minutes. I think that was the only time we cried simultaneously. During the next two months as we began to live with the genetic facts, our individual strong and weak moments usually alternated so that one was able to bolster the other.

Our immediate concern was what to tell our parents. Paul's mother was anxiously awaiting her first grandchild whom she had only seen through the hospital nursery window. While Paul was bringing me home from Booth, my parents had arrived after a five-hour drive from Connecticut. Since Dr. Chandler's suspicions were only *that*—suspicions—we decided on the way home not to say anything to our families until his suspicions were either confirmed or denied. More important, we did not want to say anything until our own emotional dust had a chance to settle. If our parents noticed our concern, we wanted them to read it as concern about Cara's jaundice.

As Paul pulled into our driveway, I had a sudden sinking feeling—I had come home without our baby. I had never felt so empty. We braced ourselves and tried to smile when we explained to our parents about jaundice, how common it was in newborns and how Cara was sunbathing it away. Paul and I avoided looking at each other. I noticed him gaze out the window. I knew his thoughts and wanted to reach out and talk with him, but our decision not to discuss Cara's problem with our parents prevented me. I went on chatting lightly with our families.

Paul's mother had a return reservation on a train to New York City that afternoon. My mother tried to convince her to stay longer. "There's plenty of room, Lee. Why don't you stay?"

Paul diplomatically cut in, "That's all right, Mom. We don't know if

Cara will be released tomorrow or the next day so why don't you go on home and come back next week. After all, you have already seen her in the hospital." He desperately wanted her to leave because he found it too difficult to put on a cheerful front for her.

After she left we chatted with my parents. Mom suggested I take a nap. I wasn't tired but I welcomed the chance to get away by myself. I couldn't sleep. Thoughts cascaded through my mind. Is Dr. Chandler right? He must be mistaken. If he is right, how will our families take it? How badly will it crush Paul? And my sensitive young brother Mike, hundreds of miles away in his first year of college? He was the kind of kid who cried years ago when his boyhood hero, Sam Huff, was traded to the Washington Redskins. He was crushed, at age twelve, when he learned that two little boys from Harlem whom he had befriended didn't have fathers—not have fathers to hit grounders to them? His ideal, middle-American, apple-pie world was shattered. How would he take the news of Cara? Ironically, it turned out that my sister, whom I thought could take the situation as well as anyone, was the one who was probably most upset.

But one thought never entered my mind. That was the question that often occurs to parents of a newborn retarded child—or is planted in their minds by well-meaning family, friends or doctors—the question, "Shall we place this child in an institution?" We never considered that question. There were several reasons.

The strongest reason, I'm sure, was that "infant-mother bonding," as the child psychologists call it, had already taken place between Cara and me. In just three days that bond had been cemented. I had been awake during Cara's birth. I had immediately held her. She was constantly at my bedside, and I was breastfeeding her, or trying to.

Another reason why the thought of placing Cara in an institution never entered my mind was a newspaper story I once wrote in North Carolina. I interviewed a woman who was active in her local Association for Retarded Citizens. Her son, who had cerebral palsy, had lived in an institution briefly. She described how seriously he had regressed after he entered the institution. She and her husband were so shaken at his lapse that they brought him back home despite the hardship it placed on the whole family. That autumn conversation in her living room must have

made a strong subconscious impression on me. Though I knew intellectually that home-reared children develop better than institutionalized
ones, the interview with her forged that knowledge emotionally. I could
never "place" Cara.

While I was supposedly napping, Paul came upstairs. We rehashed
what Dr. Chandler had said. Paul looked up "Down's syndrome" in the
dictionary. It did not appear. He looked up "mongolism." That definition
was hardly comforting: "abnormal condition of a child born with a wide,
flattened skull, narrow, slanting eyes, and generally a mental deficiency.
. . . also called mongolian idiocy." That definition just did not fit the tiny,
pretty baby we had held over the last three days.

Paul kept repeating, "I have this feeling that Cara is dead. It's as if they
took Cara away, the Cara who was just born to us, and replaced her with
another baby."

Paul was already preparing to accept Dr. Chandler's suspicions. His
grief was a natural and healthy reaction to the pediatrician's words. I was
not yet prepared to mourn. I preferred to hold on to a hope that Dr.
Chandler could be wrong. Though I understood Paul's grief, I did not
fully share it. Over the next few weeks, as genetic tests proved Dr. Chandler's suspicions correct, the emotion of grief evaded me. I was certainly
deeply saddened, but the emotion which crowded out the others was anger. I would look down at that sweet little face nestled in the crook of my
elbow and silently scream, "Goddamn it, it is so *unfair*! She did not even
ask to be born, much less to have a mental handicap. It is so goddamn
unfair to her."

Late that afternoon my father suggested going out to dinner. A fine
idea, we all thought, but first we would go by Booth so I could nurse
Cara.

When the elevator let us off at the second floor, I gazed past the nurses'
station to the nursery where Cara was sleeping, knees pulled under her,
fanny up in the air, headband around her eyes, naked pink under the
bilirubin lamp.

Paul and I put on hospital gowns and entered the nursery. One of the
nurses said Cara had been offered milk and water from a bottle but she
drank little. I picked her up and her eyes opened. I fumbled with the hospital gown to unbutton my blouse. Cara still did not seem hungry. I

stroked her cheek and chin and offered her the nipple again and again. She seemed to suck a little at a time. After about twenty minutes of this frustration, I gave up. The nurse said she would offer a bottle again later. I said I'd come back after dinner.

Months later I met a mother of a Down's child who took a month to learn to suck. I have enormous respect for that mother's patience and diligence, but had she strolled in to the Booth nursery at that moment and told me her tale, I would have burst into tears.

I had so much wanted to nurse my new baby. I hated the possibility of not being able to. I was jealous of the bottle. What if she takes to the bottle and gets hooked on it rather than on me, I thought. It is, after all, easier for a baby to learn to suck on a bottle than on the breast.

We rejoined my parents and went to a busy steak house. Dad said it was one of the best steaks he'd ever had. Paul returned several times to the salad bar. He seemed a bit more relaxed, or else he was becoming a better actor. Socially, dinner went well. Everyone talked happily. I even enjoyed my meal in spite of the fact that I was terribly uncomfortable because my milk had come in and I felt bloated. Please, Cara, I silently pleaded, catch on to this nursing routine soon.

We returned to Booth after dinner. By this time visiting hours had begun so my parents could come up to the second floor to see Cara through the nursery window. They were beaming as they stepped off the elevator. Evelyn Grossman, the midwife who attended Cara's birth, was at the nurses' station. I introduced her to Mom and Dad and mouthed a hushed aside worthy of a Shakespearean actress: "They don't know yet." I had not discussed Dr. Chandler's suspicions with Evelyn but I was sure she must know something. Evelyn just smiled.

Paul and I grabbed the green gowns again and went into the nursery. We brought Cara to the window to meet her new grandparents. Her eyes blinked at them. Dad took a picture through the window. I again tried to nurse her. She did a bit better this time but still did not take much milk. Another nurse said she had taken a little bottle milk while we were at dinner. At least she won't starve, I thought.

We went to bed early but Paul and I lay awake talking and crying. We went over the same ground again and again until it became a well-worn path. But Paul tossed out a new idea.

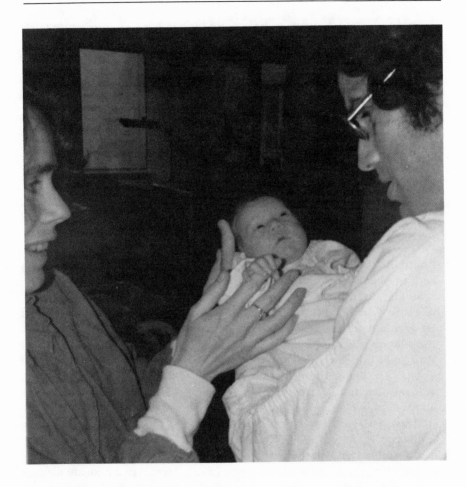

"Don't you think it would be a good idea to have another child fairly soon? I want so much to have a normal child, one we can really talk with, one who'll ask questions."

I agreed. Even before Cara's birth we had thought we wanted two children. Another thought came to me. "Maybe we should think of having two more because one might seem like an only child."

"What do you mean?" Paul looked very skeptical.

"Well, if we have another, that child might seem like an only child because its relationship to Cara probably won't be like that of normal siblings. But if that one had another brother or sister, it might be a more normal situation."

"I see what you mean. Maybe." That was a decision we both knew was far off. We did not realize it, but we were making assumptions about Cara's future which were unfounded.

The next morning we dropped my parents off at Mass on our way to Booth. As they got out of the car, Paul, who hadn't practiced his Jewish faith in twenty years, said, "Please say a prayer for Cara."

Sunday morning was particularly quiet in the nursery. While I tried to nurse Cara, Paul distracted himself by staring through a glass wall at Dr. Franklin, who was about to circumcise a three-day-old boy. Suddenly the silence was shattered by his screams. Cara seemed undisturbed, but Paul and I cringed.

After Dr. Franklin finished the circumcision, he came in to see us. It was the first time I had seen him since Dr. Chandler had spoken to us about Cara.

"Have you heard what Dr. Chandler thinks about Cara?" I asked him immediately.

He nodded and pushed strands of gray hair off his forehead. He sat down silently. John Franklin has none of the stereotyped bedside manner some physicians are reputed to have. Throughout my pregnancy and Cara's delivery, which he periodically checked in on, I had liked his quiet, direct approach. I had ultimate confidence in his professionalism. And I liked him as a person. He could discuss newspaper coverage of local politics as well as IUDs. He is a Harvard-trained obstetrician from Tennessee who wears turtleneck sweaters one day and three-piece suits the next. He is more concerned with the well-being of poor, unwed pregnant teenagers than with making $200,000 a year in the suburbs. He lives in a row-house on a modest block in Germantown, a part of Philadelphia splotched with pockets of severe poverty as well as nicely renovated blocks.

"How is she doing?" Dr. Franklin asked.

"Not nursing very well."

"That will come."

"You've seen hundreds of newborns. Do you think there is anything abnormal about Cara?" I asked him.

"She looks perfectly all right to me," he replied.

That was the brightest ray of hope I had heard in the last twenty-four hours. I snatched it. But the mental seesaw kept going up and down. From moment to moment the odds changed—leaning toward Franklin; no, Chandler may be right (after all, he is the pediatrician); yet Franklin oversees about 1,400 births a year at Booth. Back and forth, back and forth.

That weekend was the most trying of our lives. Paul alternately paced and tried to hold casual conversations with Mom and Dad. He would duck off to read *The Boys of Summer* from time to time. I noticed the book in the bathroom and, not having read it or knowing anything about Jimmy Erskine at that point, I thought, "Strange, I wonder why he's reading that again?" But the question soon passed out of my mind and I forgot to ask Paul. Several days later he showed me the Erskine chapter.

Paul went into Cara's room, freshly ready for her arrival, yet eerily empty. He stared at the wallpaper I had recently hung. It has a bright alphabet pattern: "A" and a picture of an apple; "B" and a butterfly.

He confessed that night, "I was looking at that wallpaper in her room. I wonder if she will ever be able to read those letters."

I had no answer. Neither of us knew her potential. Neither of us knew that in two years she not only would point to the picture next to the "T" and say, "tur-tull," but would also be able to recognize each letter and recite the whole alphabet.

Sunday dragged on. Paul kept from climbing the walls by shuttling me back and forth to Booth. Cara's nursing had hardly improved, but she was getting a little nourishment from bottles. Between nursing attempts we tried to concentrate on the Sunday papers.

After breakfast on Monday Dad left for home. Cara's bilirubin count was not good enough Sunday for Dr. Chandler to be willing to release her, though the jaundice was diminishing. We still did not know when she would be able to come home. Paul decided to go to work. About nine o'clock Mom and I drove to Booth. Once again I had the eerie feeling of visiting my new baby when I knew she should be home with us.

I hadn't even tied the hospital gown when Theresa Carr, the warm, gray-haired nursery nurse, came toward me with a beaming smile.

"Dr. Chandler says you can take Cara home today, dear. We took another bilirubin test this morning and it's okay. He also made arrangements for you to see Dr. Gary Carpenter at Jefferson Medical College. He's a geneticist and he can do the tests for you."

"Great. How soon?"

"Well, he'll be there until eleven this morning."

"Good, I'll just have time to try to nurse Cara and get there in time." Events were suddenly speeding up. After such a painfully slow, inactive weekend, this new pace encouraged me.

Cara's appetite was far from voracious but I wasn't discouraged. We were going home at last. "Don't worry, dear," Mrs. Carr assured me, "she'll catch on. She'll nurse much better at home." We bundled her up in her own clothes and blankets. No more hospital garb. I rushed to the hall to tell Mom, "She can come home," and dashed back into the nursery.

"Oh, Mrs. Carr, where is Jefferson? All I know is that it is somewhere downtown." We had lived in Philadelphia only four months. Mrs. Carr smiled and handed me a torn-off corner of a yellow, outdated nursery census. On the back she had pencilled the geneticist's name, location and time. I jammed it in my pocket, thanked her and signed some discharge papers.

"Don't worry, dear, she'll be all right." I felt if Mrs. Carr said Cara would be all right, she would.

As I hurried out of the nursery with Cara, I realized I hadn't told Mom. "Oh, my God," I thought, "Mom thinks we're going straight home. What a way to break the news to her."

We had to wait a moment for one of the nurses to grab her coat. Booth's policy stipulates that a nurse must carry the baby downstairs and to the car. In the lobby, Ann, the clinic nurse who had taken my blood pressure and weight on all my prenatal checkups, rushed up to me.

"Oh, Martha, what a great delivery you had! I looked through the delivery room window and you looked like you were lying on a beach like this." She bent her elbow and put it behind her head. We laughed.

"Yes, it was really easy," I said. She obviously didn't know about Dr. Chandler's suspicions. I wondered if any of the other nurses and midwives did.

Our departure scene was not a standard one with Nurse handing Baby to Mother and Father starting the car. Instead, the nurse handed Cara to my mother and I started the car. I let the engine idle and I said, "Mom, we're not going straight home. They want to do some other tests on Cara at a hospital downtown." She looked up from gazing at Cara to me.

"But I thought she was over the jaundice enough to come home."

"Well, she is. It's not the jaundice. I really didn't want to tell you this way, but I just learned they can do these tests this morning, so I have no choice. Dr. Chandler thinks Cara may have a form of mental retardation. He is not sure, but these tests will find out."

"But nothing seems wrong with her," Mom said, looking down at Cara in her lap.

"He thinks she may have Down's syndrome, which is mongolism. He notices some signs of it, but not others. He says her muscle tone is floppy, which is one sign, and that her eyes have an almond shape, which is another. But she doesn't show other signs like a heart murmur or a single crease in her palm. Since we're not sure I didn't tell you right away. I wanted to bring Cara home first and let you have a chance to hold her and observe her and break it to you slowly. And I thought if you first had a chance to be around her, you might be able to tell if you thought she looked any different from a normal baby. For instance, when Dr. Chandler told us about the slanted eyes, Paul thought that might be just familial because Janet [my sister] has slightly almond-shaped eyes."

"Yes, and so does your cousin Steve. So it might be a family thing," Mom said.

"It might be. But that's what these tests will show."

Mom's reaction to this sudden news was typical of her—no tears, no hysterics. But like me, she immediately began to deny the awesome possibility and look for positive, "normal" signs in Cara. And I looked to my mother to reaffirm my hope that this was all a nightmare.

It took about thirty minutes to negotiate morning traffic from Booth to downtown. It was the only time I recall since I was sixteen that my mother rode with me without cautioning me not to follow the car ahead too closely. There wasn't a word or a gasp from her about my driving. She later told me she was amazed that I could drive so coolly in city traffic under the circumstances.

I was looking for any hopeful sign that day. Even the rare vacant parking space directly across from the Jefferson entrance seemed a good sign. Logic had abandoned me these last few days. I equated a free parking space with the good fortune that Cara's tests would prove negative.

It was a biting cold day. We covered Cara's face with a blanket as we dashed across the street. I thought how strange it was to bring a five-day-old baby to a medical college, but the blasé med students in the elevator didn't even notice. At the seventh floor we got off and turned left where a sign pointed, "genetic counseling."

"We're here to see Dr. Carpenter," I told the secretary. She asked my name and said he'd be ready in a few minutes.

When he strode down the hall, Dr. Carpenter reminded me of a lanky Gary Cooper–Jimmy Stewart type. Dr. Chandler later told me, "I sent you to Gary Carpenter because he is a human being as well as a good doctor."

"Even babies born on the Fourth of July leave the hospital all bundled up. But on a day like today, I guess she needs it," he said as we peeled off Cara's layers of blankets.

TWO

"Do You See Those Tiny Spots?"

Dr. Carpenter began directly with an explanation of what Down's syndrome is—a genetic accident. He stressed that nothing went wrong during pregnancy. Nothing a mother eats, drinks, breathes, does or feels causes Down's syndrome. It is caused by a genetic accident near the time of conception. No mother should feel guilty about what she did or didn't do during pregnancy, because Down's syndrome is not her fault.

A person with Down's syndrome has an extra chromosome in every cell of the body. A chromosome is a microscopic, thread-like bundle of genetic material within every human cell. It carries hereditary information in the form of genes that determine the growth, development and characteristics of each person. Just how that extra chromosome turns up to cause Down's syndrome is still a mystery a century after the British physician J. Langdon Down first systematically described it in 1866. Down's syndrome takes its name from him. Its association with an extra chromosome was suggested by P. J. Waardenburg in 1932. Until 1959, many notions floated about as to its cause—glandular imbalance, virus, parental alcoholism, tuberculosis, a cultural regression. But in that year, Drs. Jerome Lejeune, Raymond Turpin and Marthae Gauthier published their findings that Down's syndrome is the result of a chromosomal anomaly, the extra one in every cell of the body. Their discovery was a major step in removing parental guilt surrounding the birth of a Down's syndrome baby.

The extra chromosome produces a variety of clinical signs: slanted or almond-shaped eyes; a small head; poor muscle tone; a flat bridge of the nose; a fold of skin over the inner corner of the eye (called an epicanthic fold); respiratory or heart disorders; a tongue too large for a relatively small mouth cavity; Brushfield spots (named for Dr. Thomas Brushfield, who first noted them in 1924), which are tiny, light-colored specks encircling the iris of the eye; a single crease across the palm of the hand (called a simian crease); short, stubby fingers; and slower than average mental development. These are a few of about fifty observable signs of Down's syndrome. Usually only a few signs appear in any one individual. Why the extra chromosome causes these particular signs is not known.

Every cell in the human body contains tiny chromosomes in the cell's nucleus. There are twenty-three matching pairs of chromosomes, a total of forty-six, in each normal cell. Geneticists have numbered these twenty-three pairs for purposes of identification and classification under a microscope. A person with Down's syndrome usually has forty-seven chromosomes, with the extra one added to the twenty-first pair. This condition is called Trisomy 21 and is the type of Down's syndrome that 95 percent of Down's syndrome people have. The other 5 percent have either a type called translocation or mosaicism.

In translocation, the extra chromosome is attached to another chromosome or may break off and attach itself to another pair such as the fourteenth or twenty-first pair. Unlike Trisomy 21, translocation is a condition that occurs when one parent is a carrier of a particular gene. That parent doesn't have a third chromosome in the twenty-first pair, but one of his chromosomes in that pair is attached to another, giving him only forty-five chromosomes. This doesn't alter the parent's physical appearance or intelligence. In fact, the parent usually doesn't know he or she is a carrier until a Down's syndrome child is born and the parent is subsequently tested.

Mosaicism, an even more rare form of Down's syndrome than translocation, occurs when some cells have forty-six chromosomes and others have forty-seven. Skin cells, for instance, may have forty-six chromosomes while blood cells have forty-seven.

These three kinds of Down's syndrome can be described as involving faulty chromosome distribution. "How does it happen?" is usually the first question of anguished parents. The answers are clinical, and not of much comfort, to parents of a newborn Down's syndrome child, but they are necessary to a fuller understanding of the condition.

A chromosome is composed of thousands of genes and other chemicals that are crucial to a person's development. The genes have often been compared to a computer that programs the code the body needs to grow and function. The genes determine whether we have blue or brown eyes, how tall or short we are, whether we are female or male, angular or built like a barrel.

Genes come from both our parents. The genes in one chromosome must work harmoniously with corresponding genes on its partner chromosome for normal development to occur. When a third chromosome appears, that balance is thrown out of kilter. It is as if two equally weighted children on a seesaw were joined by a third child who jumped on one side. This out-of-balance condition produces the differences in physical and mental development in a person with Down's syndrome.

But where does this third chromosome come from? Scientists are not positive, but they speculate that the imbalance begins about the time of conception. A mother's egg contains twenty-three chromosomes and the father's sperm contains another twenty-three. When the sperm fertilizes the egg, one cell is formed—a fertilized egg containing forty-six chromosomes matched in twenty-three pairs. That fertilized egg grows from one cell to many as the cell divides first into two identical cells, then into four, then into eight, and so on. As this process, called cell division, rolls along, the cells become heart, lungs, eyes, skin and bones of the growing fetus. Whenever a cell divides into two, the chromosomes must also divide, each making an exact replica of itself.

Trisomy 21 occurs when the cells don't divide evenly. One of the two new cells gets an extra chromosome while the other is deprived of one. Scientists do not yet know why or precisely when this uneven distribution of cells occurs. One theory holds that the egg and sperm may be perfectly healthy but when they get together, the very first cell division of the newly fertilized egg is faulty—one new cell gets three chromosomes and the other only one. That single chromosome cell cannot function and dies, leaving the other cell with three chromosomes to pass on to each new cell as cell division proceeds.

Dr. Carpenter explained that the observable signs of Down's syndrome can appear individually in any infant. In other words, floppy muscle tone or slanted eyes in a five-day-old infant is not conclusive proof of Down's syndrome. The only way to know for certain, he said, is to take a tiny blood sample and examine the baby's chromosomes under a high-powered microscope.

As he explained this, he took us into an examining room where several student nurses were waiting. Dr. Carpenter asked if I would mind if they observed Cara's examination. "No," I said as an automatic courtesy response, but somehow I felt their presence was an invasion of privacy at a very delicate time.

He stripped Cara down to her diaper. He bent his elbow and turned the palm of his large hand upward. He placed Cara on her stomach across his flat palm. Her head drooped downward.

"Usually the reflex is to hold up the head," Dr. Carpenter commented to no one in particular.

He listened—it seemed interminably—to her heart. "No, I don't hear a heart murmur. And I've listened very closely for one," he said, looking directly at me.

He examined the palms of her hands, which showed tiny patterns of dishpan-hands-type wrinkles. And he looked at her similarly wrinkled feet. Then he looked at her eyes. He looked closely and long.

"Do you see those tiny spots like a little string of pearls in the iris?" he asked me.

I looked carefully and at first could not distinguish anything. Then I saw them. Yes, they were like a string of pearls, each far tinier than a pinhead. More like a pinpoint.

"Those are called Brushfield spots," Dr. Carpenter said. This was suddenly getting too specific for me. Floppy muscle tone, heart murmurs, palm creases, slanted eyes—these were all things I had seen or heard of in normal children. But this specific name, Brushfield spots, was too foreign, too clinical-sounding, too damn dangerous. For the first time, I realized that Dr. Chandler's suspicions might well be true. This sign, with a doctor's name attached to it, was awesome. Possibility was edging too close to probability.

"Well, what do you think? What are her chances of having Down's syndrome?" I asked Dr. Carpenter.

"I never like to say for certain from a physical examination. She has some signs and not others. But that's why chromosome studies are done.

They are conclusive. I'm going to take a blood sample from her. I'll take as little as possible and still have enough for the study. If you'd rather not watch me take the sample, you might want to wait in the hall."

Until that moment my mother had watched the examination silently. "Yes, I think I'd rather wait outside," she said, surprising me. I hadn't realized how much this was affecting her until then. But how could it not?

I stayed. I have never been squeamish about blood and I certainly did not want to leave Cara even for a moment. When Dr. Carpenter stuck the needle in her skinny arm, my five-pound, seven-and-a-half-ounce bundle howled. Her claret red blood slowly filled a five-cc. vial.

"That should do it," Dr. Carpenter concluded as he put a bandaid on her arm. "You can get her dressed now." My hands shook as I fumbled with her tiny clothes. Dr. Carpenter explained the laboratory process for the blood sample: the white blood cells would be separated from the red ones. The white cells would be put in a culture to grow. Because chromosomes can be seen only in dividing cells, their growth would be stopped at the point of cell division and stained with a substance that makes them easier to photograph under a powerful microscope. The photographs of individual chromosomes would be cut out and arranged according to size, from largest to smallest, in their twenty-three pairs. This picture is called a karyotype.

The growing, staining and photographing of the cells is a slow and delicate process. It would take three to four weeks, Dr. Carpenter said. That seemed like infinity to me, but in retrospect, I think it is probably better to have that much time to adjust to the probability of Down's syndrome than to have the fact suddenly dumped on you, as has happened to many parents who have been told flatly, even before leaving the hospital delivery room, that their child has Down's syndrome because visible signs are present.

Later that afternoon Paul spoke with Dr. Carpenter on the phone. He asked, "Do you have an opinion about whether or not Cara has Down's syndrome?"

"Well, I don't like to give an opinion unless I'm asked. And it seemed that your wife wasn't really pressing me for my opinion this morning. But since you're asking me, I'd have to say that in my opinion, your baby probably does have Down's syndrome." Dr. Carpenter added that only the tests are definitive, but he had examined so many babies he could be virtually certain of his opinion.

So the long wait for The Definitive Answer began. Days of hoping against probability. Knowing Down's syndrome was more probable than possible, I still leaned toward the hopeful side of the seesaw. Days of frustrating waiting. Days of Paul's being up and my being down. Vice versa.

Before Cara was born, Mom had offered to come and stay for a week right after we came home from the hospital. Now that she knew the possibility of Down's syndrome, she offered to stay on indefinitely, even though she had planned to join Dad on a business trip to Puerto Rico the following week. She was of immense help that first week both in giving me time to rest and in pure emotional support to Paul and me. One evening I walked into the kitchen and found Paul wiping tears from his eyes. Mom had been trying to comfort him. Paul and my mother can argue furiously over politics but they share a strong bond that, I suspect, goes back to the first traumatic week of Cara's life.

The first bright sign of that week came the afternoon Cara came home. I sat on the sofa to nurse her. For the first time her little cheek muscles began pulling with some determination. Three tugs in a row, then a long rest; five pulls, a rest; one pull, rest, squirm; four pulls . . . Suddenly she was catching on to this sucking business and I began to count. She got to 43 consecutive pulls and was actually drinking milk! I felt I was witnessing a miracle. She rested and burped before starting in again. Mom sat next to us and smiled. I was so excited by Cara's new ability to nurse that I counted as if I were in a trance. Her highest count was 118 consecutive pulls and swallows. She had learned. She was strong enough and determined enough to work at nursing. I hadn't been happier since the morning of her birth.

Each time I recall that vivid memory, I realize that it was the first of Cara's many miraculous achievements. With equal determination, she would learn to crawl and walk and jump and hop and read—not with the casual facility of most children, but with a dogged determination and repetitive practice that was her own unique style.

From that afternoon until she was weaned at twelve months of age, Cara nursed well. She never used a bottle. When offered one, she refused.

At five months, she began drinking juice and water from a cup I held for her. A few months later she was holding her own cup, with the usual amount of infant spills. Nursing gave me great pleasure but its greatest benefit, I firmly believe, was in helping Cara develop the strong mouth and jaw muscles necessary to later speech development.

Four days after Dr. Carpenter took Cara's blood sample, a secretary from his office called. "I'm sorry, Mrs. Jablow, but we'll need another blood sample from your daughter. We didn't get enough white cells in the sample to grow. Could you please bring her in again Monday for another sample?"

"Of course," I said, trying to keep the frustration and anger out of my voice. Hell, that will delay the results another week, I thought.

The immediate problem was how, when, whether to tell our relatives about Cara. We persuaded Mom by the end of the week that she should go along with Dad to Puerto Rico. We had loved having her, but staying with us instead of going with Dad seemed useless. She thought it best not to tell Dad yet. Why spoil his week in the sun with news which might turn out to be moot in the long run? she reasoned. Paul and I agreed with her. But we couldn't imagine how she could conceal her fears about Cara from Dad for a week. She apparently managed to do so because Dad later said he suspected nothing. Mom undoubtedly called on her acting techniques from her college stage days.

If we delayed telling Dad until Dr. Carpenter's tests were complete, we decided, we would also delay telling the rest of my family. But Paul's mother presented another dilemma. She would be coming back the following week. Should we tell her before the test results were in, or keep up the charade? Her travel plans complicated matters. She was planning to go to Florida to visit her sister and would be there when the tests were finished. We didn't want to tell her over the phone then. Yet why tell her now and cause her worry that might be unnecessary? When we told her I was pregnant, she was as happy as Paul or I had ever seen her. Most of her friends had older grandchildren, some even in their teens, while Cara was her long-awaited first. She glowed when she first saw Cara in the hospital. "I wanted to get her her first dress," she had said as I opened a silver box containing a pale blue organdy dress with an embroidered white eyelet pinafore.

Could we shatter her joy with a single sentence: "The doctor thinks Cara may be retarded"? Paul and I discussed this over and over again. Finally Paul concluded that it was best to level with her. Tell her the possibility, that it was only a possibility, but tell her now. If we wait and tell her after she returns from Florida, we'll have lost our credibility, and she might always worry that we're holding something back from her.

Paul's mother came down the following week. Paul was at work. For most of the afternoon, she and I chatted about the baby gifts which were arriving daily, many from her friends whom I'd never met. She held Cara like any proud grandmother. The longer this happy scene went on, I felt, the more difficult it would be to tell her. I also felt that telling her would be easier for me than for Paul simply because there is more distance between a woman and her mother-in-law than between a son and mother. I knew from our talks about how to tell her that Paul would have mustered the strength to tell her, but I knew that it would have been very difficult. He had enough other burdens on his mind, so I decided to tell her before Paul came home for dinner. And I suspected Paul would prefer it this way.

We were sitting in the living room after Cara had napped and nursed. Cara was in my lap and Lee was in a chair to my left.

"Lee, there's something about Cara that has the doctors worried," I began. As I continued slowly to explain that mental retardation was a possibility, her eyes clouded and she grasped my hand tightly.

"Oh, no. Oh, dear, how sad for you," was her first response. Her first concern was for Paul and me. But she soon switched gears, as we all had when first told of the Down's syndrome possibility, to the optimistic. "But maybe the tests won't show it. We'll pray they're wrong."

Here was an ecumenical scene indeed—my Jewish mother-in-law, my Wasp-converted-to-Catholic mother and my Irish Catholic father praying for this tiny Russian, Polish, English, German, Irish infant who had an extra chromosome.

Paul's mother, like all the rest of our friends and family members, rallied to give us tremendous support at this most discouraging time. There was never a mention of "Why don't you give the baby up for adoption or put her in an institution?" as I have heard other parents of Down's syndrome babies say they've been told by relatives or friends.

Each day of the three-week wait for Dr. Carpenter's results brought a new card of congratulations or a new baby gift. Many of the messages were sadly ironic because the sender didn't know of our "problem." Paul's Aunt Sue had knitted a yellow blanket, sweater and cap which arrived shortly before Cara was born. The accompanying note read, "May the coming event be the joy of your life."

Our dear friend Jim Bready typed a welcome-to-the-world letter to Cara from his editorial office at *The Baltimore Evening Sun*:

People will sometimes be asking you about your name. In the best tradition of your forefathers and foremothers, don't abbreviate your answer. Tell 'em about caracul, the sheep from a lake region high in the Pamirs. Tell 'em about the black-haired Irish. How do Turkish (in which kara=black) and Irish come together? Easy. In geography class they'll instruct you in the Galicias. The one in Spain speaks for itself—we Celts may have been there before we ever crossed over into the northern isles. The one in Poland is sort of doubtful, etymologically. But Galatia in Asia Minor is solid, very solid. One of the books you'll come across contains an epistle to the Galatians by a historical figure named Paul. I'll break off in a hurry, before your father throws something at me. Kathleen's a nice name, too, and altogether genuine. When you get to Ireland you'll find the alphabet there has no K in it—the world's often like that, full of differences. Having the best sort of parents, you'll learn how to live with small nuisances, and change the big ones.

Oh, what a cruel hoax this could be! Jim like everyone else was assuming our newborn was a bright child with a limitless future. It was a natural assumption but I fretted that its irony would be embarrassing for those who made such assumptions. Letters like these were alternately warming, amusing and troubling.

Though we had decided not to tell anyone other than Paul's mother and mine until we heard from Dr. Carpenter, Paul found it increasingly difficult to go to work with a proud-new-father grin. He soon confided to a close friend and superior that if his performance was off, the worry over Cara was the cause. His editor suggested Paul take some time off, if it would help, but Paul felt it was better to keep working, to stay busy.

The day finally arrived as we knew it would. A sunny Friday, March 22, 1974. It was noon and I was in the kitchen when I heard Paul's key turn in the front door. There could be only one reason he would come home in the middle of the day. Dr. Carpenter had called him. And Paul wouldn't have come home just to tell me that Dr. Chandler's suspicions were a washout. That could have been done in one happy phone call, news to be celebrated later. No, he came home to tell me what we had feared, what our fear had prepared us for—the confirmation that Cara was mentally retarded.

There were no sobs or tears. I read it all in Paul's face. We held on to each other. Very little could be said.

"Let's get out of here. Let's take a drive," Paul suggested. We had a quick lunch of tuna-and-macaroni salad then wrapped Cara up and drove out to rural Montgomery County to a park beyond Valley Forge. We said little during the drive but we both felt a sense of relief. At least we now knew for certain. As Paul put it, "Now we can get on with the business of raising her and get beyond this genetics crap." He never had much patience for lengthy explanations of chromosomes and cell division.

We got out of the car and carried Cara to a low stone wall where we sat and gazed across a duck pond. A lovely scene, any observer might have thought. A new family. Spring. The beginning of a new life. Yet for us that new life was full of uncertainty. We knew nothing of the potential of this new, little being. We held vague visions of "retardation." We knew nothing about how to help Cara, what educational or physical programs might help her develop, what health problems she might have. The three of us on that stone wall might well have been sitting on a remote island in an ocean of ignorance. At that moment, we were merely survivors.

We had one lifeline, our love for Cara. That meant our total acceptance of her. Denial that she might be retarded was receding. In completely accepting her as she was, we accepted the fact that she would not be a child of normal intelligence. We wanted the best possible life for her, though we could not even dimly imagine what a life plan for her might be. She would carry that extra chromosome in every cell of her body for the rest of her life and we would make her life as happy and productive as possible.

That March afternoon grew windy. We covered Cara as best we could while we expressed these thoughts. Then we left the stone wall by the duck pond and drove home. Paul had two double martinis and helped me prepare chicken livers and mushrooms for dinner.

Once the chromosome results were known, we began calling family and friends to tell them about Cara. We called Paul's mother in Florida. She seemed well prepared to accept the sad news. She seemed further comforted by Paul's sister, who spoke encouragingly of a family she knew whose retarded boy was living happily and in good health with his family. My mother took it upon herself to tell Dad and the rest of my family. I later asked her how everyone took it. She dodged a precise description of how Dad and Mike took the news other than to say that it was the only time she'd seen Dad cry ("He felt so badly for you"), that Mike took it well enough, and that my sister Janet took it very hard. "I think if Cara had been born to her, she might have been totally crushed," Mom said. But a few weeks later when Janet came to visit, she didn't seem crushed at all. She treated Cara lovingly like any new baby.

I was worried about how my eighty-year-old grandmother would be affected. When Mom told her, Nana was saddened but not tearful. As was her style, Nana looked at the brighter side, saying that she knew Cara would receive the best care and love.

Friends responded with predictable sadness and comfort. Maggie Ray, our dear friend in Charlotte, North Carolina, wrote a few months later:

The birth of your Cara with Trisomy 21 is one of the most saddening events of the last year as I look back. I want you both to know that we shed tears and said anguished prayers for you, though nothing to compare with your own, I'm sure. Your courage and your acceptance of her have been obvious in your letters and in your voices. It's nothing less than we would expect of you—and yet we are grateful to see and feel it rather than bitterness and despair. I'm sure it's been, and will continue to be, a struggle to remain courageous and accepting. I believe that strength comes, somehow, from somewhere—and it will continue coming your way. We love you two and will love Cara, too, as you love our Betsy and Will. And we are available to share that love with you, and whatever strength we have that you can draw on at any time, whenever you need us.

Another letter from which I drew much comfort was one from my American philosophy professor and class advisor at Manhattanville College, Sister Ruth Dowd. I had written to her in April to tell her about Cara and to say that I was unable to attend a special twenty-fifth anniversary Mass for her. At that time, Cara had just begun her early intervention classes.

Your baby has been much in my thoughts and prayers. What a mixture of joy and sadness. It will be a great experience to see her develop with all the loving care surrounding her. The great gift is life and you may be sure she will never betray hers. John Dewey would surely approve of so early a schooling which is of course a widening of experience. I hope you remember his great admonition in Experience and Nature *that we must have PIETY toward experience, for experience is truly pedagogical.*

The support of faraway friends was most comforting. And the friend who always rallies in good times and bad was right there. Kathleen Sullivan (later Alioto) left her duties as a Boston School Committee member and came to Philadelphia the weekend after we learned Cara's test results. Kathleen's friendship goes back to our college days and it was for her that I chose Cara's middle name. Kathleen had taught many children with learning problems, though none with Down's syndrome. But her administrative assistant on the School Committee had taught a number of them and passed on, through Kathleen, encouraging words about their good dispositions and abilities.

Before returning to Boston on Monday morning, Kathleen accompanied Paul, Cara and me to Dr. Carpenter's office, where he showed us Cara's karyotype and took blood samples from Paul and me. He explained that, while Cara's version of Down's syndrome was not translocation and therefore not hereditary, he still wanted to test us for research purposes. Three weeks later we learned that neither of us was a translocation carrier.

As we waited for Dr. Carpenter, a middle-aged doctor with a young resident in tow approached us and took Cara's tiny hand. He neither introduced himself nor asked to look at her. He simply opened her palm and told the younger doctor that she had the simian crease of Down's syndrome. Then he left without even a thank-you.

Kathleen and Paul were appalled at his rudeness. "He acted like she wasn't even a human being, just a specimen," Kathleen said with disgust. I was still in a bit of a fog. I wasn't as impressed with his rudeness as with his ineptitude—Cara has no simian crease.

THREE

"When Can She Start?"

I noticed a stack of magazines on the floor next to my chair in Dr. Carpenter's office. On top of the stack a page was open to a picture of babies lying on floor mats. The caption said simply, "An infant stimulation program for retarded babies at Children's Hospital." No story accompanied the picture. Near the end of our talk with Dr. Carpenter, I asked about the magazine picture. "What is an infant stimulation program? Would it help Cara? How young do they take babies?"

"I really don't know much about that program, even if Children's Hospital still has such a program. But I'll have Miss Nash, our social worker, talk with you. She'll have more information."

He called in Laura Nash, an efficient, Irish-accented young woman who explained that infant stimulation or early intervention programs are designed to give retarded babies extra help in developing their bodies and senses at an early age.

"Something like the Head Start theory?" I asked.

"Yes, the earlier they get help, the farther along they'll be later on," Miss Nash said.

"That sounds great. How young do they start?"

"Well, I think most start about twelve or fourteen months. There are not too many programs around. I know there is a good one that meets on Saturday mornings in South Jersey, but that is probably a bit far for you. I'll check into what is available in your area."

When the phone rang the next day, I was honestly shocked that a social worker could act so quickly. Miss Nash said she had found a program in

Roxborough, a neighborhood only a few minutes from our home on the other side of Fairmount Park.

"The program is run by an agency called Ken-Crest. It has a good reputation. There's no waiting list. It is free. And they take babies from birth. I've spoken with their social worker, Miss Nowell, and she'd like you to call her if you are interested," Miss Nash said.

The idea that Cara could begin to receive extra help right away sent my spirits skyrocketing. From a book borrowed from Dr. Carpenter, I had been led to believe that a Down's child's development began to level off about age four or five. I therefore hoped that Cara could have the most experience possible packed into those first four years. I later learned that the statement about "leveling off" is nonsense. The "leveling off" idea grew out of data collected largely from institutionalized retarded children. It need not be that way if the child continues to be challenged at home and in good school programs. I also assumed that for *any* child these first few years were critical. I knew instinctively that such a program would be right for Cara. There was no way Paul and I alone could give her all she needed and deserved. We needed professional help. What I did not realize at the time was that we also needed the moral and emotional support that the Ken-Crest program would offer.

I called Nancy Nowell immediately. She reaffirmed the basic facts Miss Nash had told me and explained more about the program: it draws on various disciplines—developmental pediatrics, physical therapy, speech therapy, occupational therapy, psychology—to give the developmentally delayed child experiences that stimulate the whole brain and body. There were physical exercises to develop muscles necessary to sitting alone, crawling, walking. There were activities to prepare the baby to talk, to develop small muscles needed for handling a spoon or a pencil. There were activities to help the child learn self-help skills such as feeding, dressing and undressing.

"Remember," Miss Nowell stressed, "your child is more normal than not. She's going to have to learn to do the same things a normal child would do. The activities we do with our kids are the same as could be done with any normal child. It's just that we do them over and over, with more intensity, because these kids need more help. And we're concerned

with the whole child. Their emotional development is just as important as learning to feed themselves.

"If you want to know more about our program from a parent's viewpoint, I'll give you the name and number of a woman who also has a Down's syndrome child in our program. Her name is Bunny Curry," Miss Nowell added. I said I would like to call her and I'd also like to visit the Ken-Crest program. We set up an appointment for the next morning. As I hung up the phone, I felt for the first time that Cara had a definite future.

That evening I called Bunny Curry. Over the phone I envisioned her wearing a Ken-Crest T-shirt, she was such a cheerleader for the program. Her son Jamie had enrolled in the infant program when he was nine weeks old. Bunny could not have been happier with the progress he was making. She spoke of seeing another early intervention program which, she felt, couldn't compare with Ken-Crest's.

"They just left two children sitting on the potties for a half hour, just sitting there. I couldn't believe it. And the place didn't seem warm and caring. In fact it was dirty and the people seemed lackadaisical. But at Ken-Crest it's clean and the people honestly care about the babies. They're not just babysitting," Bunny said.

I valued Bunny's opinion, not only because she had a son enrolled at Ken-Crest for several months, but because she knew more about mental retardation than I. Her oldest child, then sixteen, had suffered brain damage at birth and was educable mentally retarded.* She also had two normal daughters ages four and five. When Bunny's older son was Jamie's age, there were no early intervention programs available. For sixteen years she taught him much herself and fought many battles to get him into decent school programs. But with Jamie, Bunny saw a new era dawning. By getting him off to an early start, she felt his progress would be smoother than her older son's.

I talked with Bunny for about half an hour about Down's syndrome in general. She repeated some of the same notions we had already heard: that Down's children are particularly sweet-natured and affectionate. But her statements carried more weight for me than those of a book, a physi-

---

*Educators generally designate an I.Q. range of 50 to 75 as "educable" and below 50 as "trainable" mentally retarded.

cian, or a social worker, because she was the first mother of a Down's child I had spoken with since Cara's birth.

She offered one bit of advice which resounded in my ears often over the next few years: "Talk to Cara. Talk to her all the time—when you're bathing her, changing her diaper, holding her. Tell her what you're doing: 'I'm washing your leg, Cara. I'm putting on your blue shirt.' It's really important for her speech later on. You may think you sound crazy, talking to her all the time about what's going on in your mind, but, believe me, it is very important." I have followed her advice. I now believe just as firmly as Bunny that talking to any baby is vital to later speech development. Two years later I was particularly conscious of talking to Cara's younger, normal brother when he was tiny. Talking intelligently—not using baby talk—to all babies not only gives them sounds to imitate, but it also lets them know how much you love them.

Early the next morning we bundled Cara up and headed for Ken-Crest. The sky was gray. Snow was forecast. The Ken-Crest center was located in a stone church four miles from home. The church's Sunday nursery quarters were Ken-Crest's weekday home.

The first person we met was Nancy Nowell. Thin, long-haired with wire-rimmed glasses, Nancy looked more like a hippie than a social worker. She took us into a classroom bright with toys, mobiles and wall posters and asked us to observe for a while.

Tumbling mats were all over the floor. Babies were sprawled on the mats in various positions and states of undress. The first bit of incidental information we learned about Ken-Crest was that the room was unusually warm because the children went through their activities clad only in diapers. Though it looked bizarre in March, there was a good reason: much of the infants' activity involved tactile stimulation and they responded best when stripped.

"This is your arm, Shelley," said one of the teachers as she rubbed the thin limbs of a child with a piece of terry cloth.

"This is soft, Shelley. Feel how soft. This is your foot I'm rubbing," she added as she stroked Shelley all over again with a different cloth that offered a new tactile sensation.

To the uninitiated like us, these goings-on looked fascinating but quite odd. What was this stroking doing for this little girl? In size, Shelley looked like a two-year-old but she could not sit alone. Her eyes gazed in opposite directions. She seemed to have difficulty lifting her head for more than a few minutes. Could she even understand what the teacher was telling her?

Shelley's movements were all involuntary, as if her nerves were short-circuited. Her hand touched nearby toys by accident not deliberate reaching. She had no muscle control.

Shelley also had respiratory problems. Later in the morning one of the teachers began a forty-five minute session of pounding Shelley's chest and back to loosen mucus in her chest. The pounding looked harsh but it did not hurt Shelley because the teacher cupped her hand, forming a suction, rather than pounding with a flat palm. After forty-five minutes of respiration therapy, Shelley was placed in a sitting position to help her cough up the loosened mucus.

On the other side of the room, fourteen-month-old Danny sat on the floor with a cushion supporting his back because he could not sit alone. Most children sit alone about seven months of age. Danny was a handsome, normal-looking child except that his head slumped and he stared at the floor. He uttered no sounds and barely moved. A teacher moved toward him but he did not seem to notice her. She offered him a wind-up toy which grunted some musical sounds. Danny seemed moderately interested, but made no attempt to grasp the toy.

Danny's problems had no label. His birth had been complicated and difficult. His first year of life had been vegetable-like. He did little but lie on his back and showed no interest in sitting or crawling on his own. From the time he entered the Ken-Crest program at age thirteen months, however, Danny had been making tremendous strides. By the time he was four, he was talking, behaving, and relating to people at a near-normal level. At age five, he could print his own name. But without a crystal ball for Danny's future, I saw that first day only a pathetic, lethargic baby.

The teacher moved from Danny to another child named Tia, a delicately thin girl whose huge brown eyes radiated from the center of a beautiful face. The teacher began massaging Tia's arms and legs. Tia seemed unable to move on her own. She was Shelley's opposite. Rather than involuntarily moving, Tia lay in a flexed position. Her hands were tightly closed, her knees bent, and her arms close to her body. To relax her body and encourage her to reach for objects around her, the teachers did a series of "range of motion," or stretching, exercises with her. They carefully straightened her arms and legs and unbent her elbows and knees to loosen her joints.

As I watched these children I wondered, "What will this program do for Cara?" She had slept and eaten contentedly for her first month of life. She seemed to have none of the problems these other children had. They appeared—to me—more severely handicapped than what we had expected a Down's syndrome baby to be. Just as I was thinking these thoughts, in walked a tall man carrying his son. The teachers burst into "Happy Birthday to You!" The father beamed. One-year-old Mark took it all in nonchalantly.

Mark had Down's syndrome. He had begun the Ken-Crest program when he was a month old. I couldn't help but watch Mark for clues to what Cara might be like a year from that moment. After Mark was undressed he went to work. Birthday boy or not, he had a routine to perform like the other babies. Mark could sit alone. He was placed at a low table in a tiny chair whose sides kept him from wandering. He was given brightly colored wooden blocks and balls not much larger than lima beans. His job was to pick them up one at a time and place them in a cup. A cautious mother might worry that a baby Mark's age would pop them into his mouth, but Mark clearly understood his task. It was easy for him to pick up the objects by scooping them up with all his fingers into the palm of his little hand, but the activity's goal was to develop the fine motor skill of picking up small objects with the index finger and thumb (we later learned this was called an inferior pincer skill), so a teacher held Mark's hand with his three other fingers curled into his palm, leaving only his index finger and thumb free to pick up the balls and blocks.

I was fascinated watching Mark's concentration when Bunny Curry walked in carrying Jamie. Chubby, blond, very fair-skinned, Jamie looked like the classic Down's syndrome children we had seen in Dr. Carpenter's book. Bunny was out of breath and talked rapidly. She had rushed through forty-five minutes of traffic from the opposite side of Philadelphia to get Jamie here. As Bunny talked to the teachers about Jamie's activities, her trust in them and their concern for Jamie became obvious. They talked about simple things, how he was sleeping and eating, but the tone was similar to a conversation among close family members about a loved child.

After Jamie was stripped down, his program began. Like many retarded children, Jamie's muscular development had been slow. Most children crawl about seven months of age. At one year, Jamie could not. His favorite position was lying on his back. Before he could learn to crawl, his shoulder and arm muscles needed strengthening. One of the teachers plopped Jamie on his stomach and caught his attention with a jingling toy. Jamie wanted the toy passionately. His arms waved. His legs kicked. The teacher held the toy above him and slightly out of his reach. To grab the toy Jamie had to support himself with his left arm while reaching with his right, thereby strengthening that left shoulder.

Jamie and Mark gave me a sense of what Cara would be doing in this program. And these two little boys gave me infinite hope. Each time they achieved a skill over the next two and a half years, I was overjoyed, not just for Jamie and Mark themselves, but also because I could foresee Cara's doing the same thing when she became their age. I was impressed with how the staff made the children work—and it was indeed hard work for them—but the most impressive thing was the warm encouragement and praise the staff gave the babies.

"That's good, Jamie. That's my man. You can get that toy." Their talking to the infants was genuine and not overly enthusiastic to the point of phoniness.

After we had observed the classroom activities for a while, Nancy introduced us to Andre Hally, the program coordinator, and Mattie Brunson, the head teacher. Their titles seemed a bit absurd because the staff acted so egalitarian. They were all working down on the floor with the infants. Andre looked as young as the two aides, Janet Wessner and Fran Ciotti. Mattie "is the expert," Nancy said. "She's the only one of us who has had children of her own."

Mattie said hello to us in a soft, husky voice that I would grow to love hearing over the coming years. She immediately took Cara and put her on a floor mat. She held Cara's hands and pulled her from a prone position to a sit. Wow, I thought, can you do that with a one-month-old baby? I had been treating Cara like a piece of fine porcelain. Mattie talked softly to Cara while she played with Cara's hands and feet. In this relaxed way Mattie was getting a feel for Cara's muscle tone.

Nancy asked us to come into her office across the hall. She offered us tea and explained the program further: it was free because it was federally funded; there was currently no waiting list; children came Monday, Tuesday, Thursday and Friday mornings; Wednesday mornings were for home visits; each family was visited about every sixth week by two staff members. Nancy gave us a form to complete if we wanted to enroll Cara.

"Since we are the first program you've looked at, I understand if you want to look further," she added. But both Paul and I had good vibes about what we had seen, particularly the sure, warm way Mattie handled Cara. We enrolled Cara on the spot. If any problems cropped up, we could always withdraw her.

"When can she start?" I asked.

"Well, Monday if you want," Nancy said. A year or two later Nancy told me she was surprised at our speedy decision to enroll Cara so young. Many parents, she said, had difficulty parting, if even for a morning, with so tiny an infant.

We walked out into the snow flurries after having made this admittedly quick, intuitive decision. We did not realize at the time that we had made a major decision that would affect the rest of Cara's life. Our trust was naive yet strong. We felt that these women knew much more about helping a retarded child than we did. The more help we could get for Cara, the better. And the earlier, the better. One of the first newspaper stories I ever wrote, back in 1965, was about an early Head Start program of Lyndon Johnson's late Great Society. Though Head Start was designed for socially and economically deprived children, the same theory seemed to apply to developmentally delayed children: give them an early start, because the younger they are, the riper they are for learning. Why not one month of age? Cara might as well be exercising on a Ken-Crest floor mat as lying on a blanket at home. Certainly I could read about child development and do exercises with her, but these Ken-Crest people already seemed to know the game and would not only work with Cara but would also teach me through their home visits. Our partnership with Ken-Crest that began on a snowy March day proved invaluable for Cara. And it opened a new world for Paul and me. It gave us hope and information and support.

Many parents who do not have early intervention programs available in their communities to work diligently with their special children at home, by reading, talking to professionals, or participating in at-home programs. I have tremendous respect for these parents who go it alone. They must feel the same pride when the child accomplishes daily minor miracles, but it must be a lonely, private pride. I do not think a day passed without one of Cara's teachers' telling me about something she did that day. It may have been a tiny thing, but the staff's mention of it gave me support. It told me that they saw her as a unique little person, that they cared for her and were proud of her every achievement. When another person, particularly someone outside the family, shares that joy or can give encouragement when progress bogs down, the parent gets immense support and energy to move ahead.

The next Monday was April 1, the first day of Cara's academic career. She was one month and four days old. Her book bag was a pink and white checked diaper bag with a white satin duck on the front. Instead of pencils, it held Pampers.

Because she was the tiniest infant, Cara was placed on a flannelette blanket spread on a floor mat. Mattie constantly talked quietly to Cara as she rubbed parts of her body with differently textured cloths. She tucked Cara's arm under her side and rolled her from back to stomach. Cara's head rested on the blanket. Mattie brought a toy near Cara's head to lure her into lifting up her head. Cara did, but only for a second. This was the beginning of many exercises to build head control. Soon Mattie would place a softly carpeted cylinder under Cara's shoulders to give her additional support in lifting her head and neck from a prone position. Mattie suggested that I do the same thing at home by rolling a towel into a tight cylinder and placing it under her shoulders as she lay on the floor or in her crib.

"But only for a minute or two at first," Mattie cautioned.

In a few weeks, as Cara gained more head control, this roll would become a game. Placing the cylinder under her chest and her arms over the cylinder, I would roll her back and forth as I held her by the hips and thighs. This activity would loosen her arms, help her to stretch and relax, and encourage her to hold her head and shoulders up. She seemed to enjoy the motion of rolling as well.

Building up head control was one of Cara's first and most important goals. Like many retarded babies, Cara had floppy muscle tone and poor muscle control. It was difficult for her to hold her head steady. Mattie urged us to help her by placing her on a rolled-up blanket or across my leg as I sat on the floor. The more Cara practiced, the stronger she became. Without Mattie's encouragement I might have pampered Cara. I probably would have held her with her head nestled against my shoulder rather than holding her higher so that she was forced to support her own head. But Mattie taught us early that we must not coddle Cara. The general goal of Cara's program was to help her become as strong physically and as independent socially and intellectually as possible, while always giving her love and emotional support. The more we allowed her to do for herself, the more wholly she would develop. This was an attitude that gelled early, as early as these first head-control exercises.

Child development books generally agree that most babies roll over by themselves, from stomach to back, about three months. Cara shocked us when she rolled over alone at five weeks. On Friday, after only three days at Ken-Crest, Cara was placed on her stomach on a floor mat by Janet Wessner. Janet left Cara to work with another child for a few moments and when she returned, Cara was lying on her back.

"I'm sure I put Cara on her stomach," Janet told the other teachers. "She couldn't have rolled over, could she?" The other teachers doubted it and chalked it up to Janet's faulty memory.

No one mentioned the incident to me when I arrived to pick up Cara. But over the weekend I placed Cara on her stomach in the middle of our bed while I dressed. A moment later she was on her back. No, I told myself, she couldn't have rolled over.

I mentioned this to Mattie on Monday morning and she told me of Janet's experience Friday. Could Janet and I both be fuzzy about the same thing? We wouldn't admit that, so we all concluded that Cara was indeed beginning to roll over. She soon began performing in public, and Janet and I regained our credibility.

While this was a big step, we could not attribute it to early intervention, since Cara had been attending Ken-Crest for only three days. But it was an important sign that Cara was strong and lively. Her light weight aided her agility. By rolling over so early, she gave us a sign that she was ready for more. The Ken-Crest staff began rolling her over, from stomach to back, back to stomach, while holding her at the hip. This gave her necessary support as well as the sensation that her upper torso was rolling freely on its own.

Mattie also suggested that I frequently position Cara on her side to watch things in her crib or on the floor. This gave her an additional perspective on the world and gave her a head start on rolling either to her stomach or back.

Another activity for a baby as young as Cara was "tracking," both visual and auditory. Cara would be placed on her back and a teacher would hold a bright toy directly above her. When Cara focused on the toy, the teacher would slowly move it to one side. Sometimes Cara would follow or "track" the toy, other times she would not. Mattie and the other teachers did this repeatedly with Cara and she increasingly tracked the toy visually.*

Tracking is not simply an eye exercise but a developmental exercise for the brain. The brain is divided into two hemispheres. When the toy was held directly above Cara it was at the mid-line—like the Greenwich meridian—of the brain's two perceptual fields. As the toy was moved across the mid-line, the brain learned to coordinate the two hemispheres.

Mattie explained that some people have never mastered such coordination. They allow the dominant side of their brains to do all the work. For instance, they drive into a highway toll booth and use the right hand to toss the coin into the basket even though the left hand is closer to the basket.

Auditory tracking was similar. A jingling toy was moved from one side of Cara's head to the other. She was to follow the sound from side to side. Like visual tracking, this exercise helped to develop both sides of the brain in coordination with each other. It also could give the teacher clues to any hearing impairment. Fortunately Cara had none.

---

* Cara's visual tracking activities included vertical as well as horizontal directions.

During Cara's early weeks at Ken-Crest, I learned more about the philosophy and background of early intervention programs. I discovered this was not simply an exercise program to strengthen a baby's muscles or improve coordination, but a program concerned with the whole child. The staff put high priority on the harmony of a baby's development, a harmony in which all segments of the infant's development grow in good balance with each other. What good was improved muscle tone if, for example, the baby's emotional state was upsetting his appetite?

In practicing this philosophy of balanced growth, Cara's teachers poured all their knowledge of various child development fields as if into a blender. Out came a warm mixture that nourished the child's complex needs. It amazed me.

For a first-time mother like me, doors opened on the many mysteries of how children develop. Had Cara been "normal," I would have picked up such information casually as I observed her and read the usual child development books. But Cara's special needs plunged me into a crash course.

One of the first books the Ken-Crest staff recommended to me was *The Baby Exercise Book* by Dr. Janine Lévy. In the introduction, Dr. Willibald Nagler, chief of rehabilitation medicine at the New York Hospital–Cornell Medical Center, writes: "For a long time it was generally accepted that the development by a child was an invariant process. It was thought to be based entirely on reflex activity which depends upon the maturation of the nervous system. This meant that crawling, walking and other activities could not be influenced by the actions of others. This view is changing, however. It is now thought that factors other than reflexes are responsible for the child's motor development. He can learn, for example, by copying those close to him."

This century has witnessed the growing recognition that very young children are capable of much more than previously assumed. As early as 1907 when she opened her first school in a Rome slum, Dr. Maria Montessori recognized the capacity for learning in very young children. She believed that from birth to six years old is the most important part of life. As Montessori set up a network of "children's houses" around the world, others were discovering the potential of the very young. In 1921, the Iowa PreSchool Laboratory began studying children who entered preschool at a mean age of forty-two months. The study, which continued through 1932, found that these children showed a mean gain of sixteen I.Q. points during an eighteen-month average stay in preschool. Later tests showed that these gains could be maintained for an average of twelve years if the child stayed in school. And one of the greatest contributors to our understanding of how children learn, Jean Piaget, has demonstrated how a child's ability to abstract begins quite young and becomes more sophisticated as he grows. Piaget also showed that a child's development is cumulative, with new behaviors modifying earlier foundations.

The understanding of child development has evolved to the point where a researcher like Dr. Burton F. White can say: "Our studies show that the period that starts at eight months and ends at three years is a period of primary importance in the development of a human being. To begin to look at a child's educational development when he is two years of age is already much too late, particularly in the area of social skills and attitudes."

Meanwhile, attitudes towards the retarded were also changing. Although in the twentieth century retarded persons were no longer left to die as in ancient Greece, they were isolated from society in institutions. And Hitler sent them off to camps and ovens with others he designated less than ideal human beings. Only recently have court decisions and legislation begun to restore the retarded person's right to live in the community and receive an education equal to that of a "normal" citizen.

The two currents—increasing understanding of how infants learn and increasing acceptance of the retarded as fellow human citizens—were bound to meet. The result was early intervention programs springing up around the country in church basements, hospitals and even private homes early in the 1970s.* There were only an estimated hundred of them, of varying degrees of sophistication, when Cara began in 1974. Most often they were hard-won programs birthed by demanding parents.

---

* In 1968, the Handicapped Children's Early Education Assistance Act was enacted to stimulate the development of comprehensive educational services for children from birth to age eight. The first twenty-four grants, totalling one million dollars, were made in 1969. As of 1982, 350 programs have been funded. The act funds model programs for three years that are to be subsequently continued and replicated at the state or local level.

Seldom did public or private agencies serving the retarded organize early intervention programs on their own. They usually started when parents organized and approached such agencies for help. This was the case with Cara's program. Parents of preschool retarded children didn't want to wait until their children were seven or eight to enter "special education" classrooms in public schools. They knew instinctively that their children needed an earlier start because they were already well behind the starting line. These parents approached Ken-Crest, a Lutheran-affiliated agency with a long history of serving older retarded persons. When the program was getting organized in the early 1970s, it was modeled on the first one in the area, a program sponsored by St. John of God in South Jersey. That program, only a few years older than Ken-Crest's, also began when a group of parents sought help from an order of Irish brothers. It had no model, but was built from scratch by the demands of parents and the advice of a psychologist.

FOUR

"Let Go of Your Support Slightly"

When any child, even one as young as Cara, enters a Ken-Crest program, tests are given. The idea of "entrance exams" for babies amused me. But I soon understood that they gave the staff an idea of where each baby stood, what her strengths and weaknesses were. When the evaluations were completed, an individual program of goals was written for each infant. Dates of accomplishments and special observations were noted on the goal sheets (or "report cards," as we called them), which were shared with parents during home visits.

Cara's first evaluation was by a physical therapist. Ken-Crest had an arrangement with a physical therapist at St. Christopher's Hospital for Children in Philadelphia. The therapist evaluated each new baby and followed up with visits to the Ken-Crest center. Nancy Nowell made an appointment for us on April 19.

My sister Janet and my four-year-old niece Jennifer were visiting at the time so we all went to St. Christopher's together. Cara was not in a particularly cheery mood because it was her naptime. But she still managed to impress the therapist, Shelley Segal. Ms. Segal played with Cara on a floor mat and did bicycle peddling exercises with Cara's legs. She got a general feel for Cara's muscle tone during the fifteen-minute session with her. Like Mattie and Nancy, the physical therapist stressed to us the importance of exercising for physical development. Ms. Segal later wrote the following report:

Cara is a six-week-old white female with a diagnosis of Down's syndrome. She appeared today quite alert and performed motor skills at age-appropriate levels, including lifting head 45 degrees in prone (position), regarding mother's face, placing fist to mouth and vocalizing. A positive Moro,* stepping and placing reactions (all normal) were demonstrated. Reportedly Cara rolls prone to supine, though this feat was not observed here today. Muscle tone is good.

Mother seems very able to carry out stimulation program with Ken-Crest in which she is enrolled. Program recommendations include turning toward sound, head control, beginning tracking, placing bright colored gloves on hands, and rolling skills.

Cara is progressing very nicely according to age level skills. She will be followed through the Roxborough Infant Program (Ken-Crest).

A week later Cara was scheduled for another test, this time a psychological one. I thought a psychological test on an infant not yet two months old was a bit much, but I went along.

Psychologist Deborah Werden tested Cara at seven weeks. She wrote the following report:

Tests administered: *Bayley Scales of Infant Development; Slosson Intelligence Test for Children and Adults; Vineland Social Maturity Scale.*
Results of testing: *Cara obtained a Psychomotor Development Index (PDI) of 106 on the Bayley. She passed all motor items up to the 1.6 month level and passed none above the 4.2 month level. Her gross motor development is clearly within normal limits. Cara is able to balance her head for over 15 seconds, push herself up by her arms*

---

* "One of the most frequent and dramatic reflexes of the newborn is the Moro reflex, a vestige from our ape ancestry. If the baby is handled roughly, hears a very loud noise, sees a bright light, or feels a sudden change in position, he startles, arches his back, and throws his head back. At the same time, he flings out his arms and legs, then rapidly closes them to the center of his body, and flexes it as if he were falling. As he cries, he startles, then cries because of the startle. This reflex, normal in all newborns, tends to disappear at three or four months of age." Frank Caplan, ed., *The First Twelve Months of Life: Your Baby's Growth Month by Month* (New York: Grosset and Dunlap, 1973), p. 22.

when on her stomach and grasp an object in her hand. She produces vigorous extensions of her arms and legs and can roll from her stomach to her back. Cara is not yet able to compensate for withdrawal of support from her head or body.

On the mental scale of the Bayley, Cara's performance was significantly lower. She had a basal score of .2 months and a ceiling of 1.5 months which produces a Mental Development Index of 66. Cara would follow a visual stimulus such as a large ring horizontally for a few inches but would not track the object vertically or circularly. She would visually follow a person for several feet while the adult walked around her crib, but this tracking was not continuous. Cara's response to such sounds as a bell or a rattle consisted of a consistent eye blink and some cessation of activity; she would not turn to find the source of the noise. At this point, there is evident delay but it must be remembered that the majority of the items she did not pass at an age-appropriate level related to visual tracking. On the Slosson, Cara obtained an I.Q. of over 100; the items on this test were primarily motor items which makes this rating consistent with the PDI of the Bayley. The Vineland produces a social age of approximately two months and again the items on this test at this level are gross motor abilities which produces a rating consistent with the PDI.

Clinical impressions and summary: *Cara is an attractive baby with a well-shaped head and very good color. She is very alert and active and remained awake throughout the two-hour observation. When left alone, Cara would "coo" and visually inspect her environment. The only apparent delay at this point is her visual coordination.*

Cara wasn't the only one being tested. One warm noon in early June, I arrived at 11:30 to pick Cara up. Nancy Nowell asked me if I had a few minutes to fill out a form for a survey on parent attitudes. Nancy didn't explain it further and I didn't question the purpose of the survey. It contained forty-eight statements such as "A mother should be resigned to the fate of her child" and "My child cannot get along without me." The mother taking the survey had five choices in response: strongly agree, agree, undecided, disagree and strongly disagree.

As I took the "test," I laughed aloud at some of the ludicrous statements like "A mother should 'show off' her child at every opportunity." I circled "strongly disagree" to that one.

When I finished the test, Nancy thanked me and I assumed it was going into some bureaucratic pile of anonymous responses which some researcher would collate into some "Meaningful Assessment of Maternal Attitudes." Much later Nancy explained that the test was designed to reveal a mother's acceptance or non-acceptance of her child. The non-acceptance category was divided into three sub-categories. On "over-protection," I had scored in the first, or lowest, percentile; on "overindulgence," I had scored in the 20th percentile; and on "rejection," I had scored in the 10th percentile. On "acceptance," which had no sub-category, I had scored in the 99th percentile. That did not surprise me at all. I knew I accepted Cara just as she was—she was a very "acceptable" baby. If the psychologists who make up such tests wanted a profile of my acceptance of her, well, let them have it. I found the whole test rather superfluous.

I had been shuttling Cara to and from Ken-Crest for a month, and each noon when I picked her up, a teacher always mentioned something Cara had done that day. But I looked forward to our first home visit for an overview of her first month in school. Nancy and Janet arrived one bright Wednesday morning in May. While we had coffee, they told me how pleased they were with Cara's progress. They gave me a small sheet of white notebook paper listing six activities we should practice with Cara at home:

—Practice rolling her forward and back while holding her at the hip.

—Encourage head control by placing Cara on her stomach with her shoulders and arms over a rolled-up blanket or towel, and encourage head control by placing her across your leg while you sit on the floor or hold her high at your shoulder.

—Have Cara lie on her side to watch things around her.

—Encourage her to try to hit large objects placed on her chest when she is lying on her back. This will lead to reaching for objects.

—Have a stimulating atmosphere in her bedroom.

—Emphasize visual and tactile stimulation, especially visual tracking in

and out from the mid-line, and play with Cara while wearing brightly colored gloves; have Cara wear mittens.

"We didn't need to write down that business about having a stimulating atmosphere in her room," Nancy said after she had seen Cara's room. It was already bright with sunlight, pictures on the walls, a crib mobile of colorful fish, red and white gingham curtains, printed crib sheet and red and white checked crib bumpers. And, of course, the wallpaper.

After Janet and Nancy left, I found some cherry red fabric and sewed tiny mittens for Cara. The idea of putting mittens on a two-month-old baby in May wasn't quite as bizarre as it seemed. The mittens attracted Cara's attention to her hands and eventually taught her that those flying objects weren't UFOs but actually part of her. She would learn that she had control over them; that she could bring them to her mouth or bat them together or use them to swing at an object nearby. She would also learn, and soon, to toss the mittens off her hands.

During the hot, humid summer I continued to drive Cara to school four mornings each week. There wasn't even a summer vacation for these babies. Cara's head control improved and her upper torso muscles grew stronger. She was often placed on her stomach in front of a low mirror as an invitation to lift her head and shoulders to catch her own image.

"One of the first things I remember about Cara is that she could lift her little head up at an early age," Mattie recalled. "I couldn't believe it." But once Mattie saw her ability to lift her head, she encouraged Cara to do it more often by enticing her with a mirror or toy.

I decided to adapt the same technique at home. When we bought our house, four months before Cara was born, I thought the nine-by-fifteen-foot room at the end of the downstairs hall would make an ideal playroom. It had an adjacent lavatory and was closed to the rest of the house by French doors. While Cara attended Ken-Crest, I spent my mornings painting and papering the house. I moved the playroom project to the top of my list of priorities when I realized it could become a mini—Ken-Crest center at home. I gave the walls and ceiling a fresh coat of white paint and painted the woodwork a deep gold. I bought a rusty red carpet remnant just the right size to cover the entire floor. It is a commercial-type, low-pile carpet which still shampoos beautifully after eight years of apple juice spills, ground-in cookie crumbs, PlayDoh droppings and a few didn't-quite-make-it-to-the-potty accidents.

While Cara, and later David, were infants this room was a bonanza. It served as a giant playpen—safe, with plenty of room to crawl around, yet enclosed. If I had to be in another part of the house, I could close the French doors without Cara or David's feeling they'd been completely shut off from me. We did go through a hefty supply of Windex, however, with all those fingerprints on the door's lower panes.

I felt virtuous at having created this giant playpen since I tried to avoid using a real playpen as much as possible. I had heard that children who are left in playpens for long periods sometimes have learning problems later, and I knew that Maria Montessori abhorred overuse of playpens and cribs. I had a playpen in the kitchen in which I placed Cara for brief times when I was cooking and couldn't have her safely under foot.

In one corner of the playroom I attached a mirror to the wall just above the floorboard. When Cara was very tiny, I placed her on her stomach in front of the mirror for head-lifting exercises. Later it became a goal for crawling. I would place her several feet away from the mirror and she would gradually inch her way toward her image. I moved her starting position back a little each time to build up her crawling distance. Later still, the mirror proved useful for working on speech. When Cara was three, we hired a speech therapist to work with her one hour each Saturday morning. For many of the activities, Beverly Kaplan-Kraut sat behind Cara as they both faced the mirror. Cara imitated Beverly's sounds while watching the way her lips formed each sound.

The mirror is on the wall today. With a puffy, three-foot-square pillow in front of it, the mirror corner has become a cozy place to look at books or play with dolls. The mirror doesn't hold as much interest as it once did, and—one of these days—I shall take it down. But I'll hate to part with anything that has served such useful, happy purposes. It has literally reflected Cara's tremendous growth.

During Cara's first six months at Ken-Crest, her activities focused mainly on building head control and on offering her a cornucopia of visual and auditory stimulation. She was bombarded with sights and sounds: music boxes, squeaky toys, hand clapping, records, triangles, wood blocks, and a bell which I can still hear and see—a little red and white polka-dot bell, shaped like a mushroom, with a face painted on the handle and a hat painted on what looked like the mushroom cap. Mattie jingled that bell near one side of Cara's head as she lay on her back. Cara would turn to the sound, "visually grasp," as Mattie said, the bright little bell and follow it with her eyes and ears as Mattie moved it across her lines of vision to the other side of Cara's head. Mattie would slowly move the jingling bell in several patterns—from Cara's mid-line to each side of her head, up ninety degrees and back to mid-line, down from mid-line and back to mid-line, and in a circular arc—first eight inches from Cara's face, then twelve inches.

Activities for visual stimulation were often linked with those for motor development. Cara was placed on her stomach and encouraged to look up at a jazzy toy. Or she was supported by a rolled-up blanket under her chest and arms and invited to track a toy from side to side. Such activities helped build head control and visual tracking simultaneously. Holding her head up for a few seconds was difficult for her at first, but the bright toy moving from side to side captured her attention and she began to hold her head up for longer periods of time.

One of Cara's earliest activities—another I wasn't prepared for so early—was being held by me in a sitting position to encourage her to support her head. At two months of age, her head bobbed and flopped down to her chest. The teachers and I were cautious about not letting her head flop down too far when her head bobbed. But by being held in a sit position frequently, yet for short spans, Cara gradually developed the strength to hold her head up more steadily.

Between three and four months normal babies master reaching for and grasping objects. It is the time when parents suddenly realize that they must watch everything in the baby's immediate environment. Things too small and swallowable are elevated to high shelves. Parents' eyeglasses are swiftly wrenched from their faces by tiny hands. Mothers put away pierced earrings lest they be ripped from earlobes. But with Cara and other developmentally delayed babies, reaching and grasping would come later if these babies weren't encouraged to reach and grasp.

One of Cara's activities during those early months was to hold a rattle.

That sounds so terribly simple. Yet it was something she had to learn. A rattle had to be placed in her hand and her fingers had to be curled around the handle so she would learn to grasp it. At first her hand went limp and the rattle dropped. But after several times, she began to keep her fingers closed. Once she held on and the rattle stayed in her grip as her arms moved about naturally, she began to realize that this little purple rattle, shaped like a telephone earpiece, provided some entertaining noise.

Lightweight, soft plastic toys, like squeaky dolls or animals, were placed on Cara's chest as she lay on her back. Propped there, they were in a likely position to be reached for and, perhaps half the time, grasped. Half the time a toy was knocked off her chest only to roll across the mat, but the Ken-Crest teachers were patient "go-fers" who would cheerfully retrieve the toy and place it back on her chest.

Cara was given the Denver Developmental Screening Test when she was three months and one week old. She had reached the "grasps rattle" step normal at that age, but not the "reaches for object" step which the Denver test places between three-and-a-half and four months. Cara had reached other Denver milestones normally achieved before three months—smiles, follows to mid-line, follows past mid-line, follows one hundred eighty degrees, holds hands together, lifts head to forty-five degrees and to ninety degrees when lying on stomach, sits with head steady, rolls over and gets her chest up with arm support when lying on her stomach. In the language of the Denver, she passed "vocalizes, not crying" but failed "laughs" and "squeals."

Tests like the Denver give milestones at the ages they are normally achieved. The importance of such tests is not in judging whether the child passes or fails, but in identifying areas where the child lags and in showing which developmental steps should follow.

"With each milestone our babies would reach," Mattie often said, "at no time did we say 'okay, rest.' But we'd always go on to the next step. It's a constant learning process. When I introduce a child to a new activity, I first show him or her what we want done. Then I help the child through it and gradually decrease the help. By the time the child masters one thing, we've already started another activity for another skill.

"I believe so strongly in using the behavioral approach of setting up goals and even sub-goals, so every little effort in reaching even a sub-goal can be a success and can be praised. We genuinely were excited when they reached a goal and that's something not many normal children are exposed to. We want to make the child's learning situations as positive as possible and that's why the activities have to be broken down into tiny steps so that we can build in success for the child."

If the child's task were to bang two cubes together (a seven- to ten-month-old skill), that skill was first broken down into smaller steps: sitting up, picking up one cube, passing it from one hand to the other, picking up a second cube, holding one in each hand, and finally mastering the eye-hand coordination to bring those two cubes together in one bang.

Even sitting up was somewhat difficult for Cara. To help her sit alone, an adult would place Cara in a sitting position with her legs out straight and her hands on her knees for support, while gently supporting her at the hips to prevent her from toppling sideways. As her time span increased from ten to fifteen seconds and her back grew stronger, that assistance was gradually withdrawn. By eight months, she sat without support.

Before Cara was three months old, I never gave a thought to her walking. Walking seemed light years away during those early months when my daily concerns for her were eating, sleeping, bathing, rolling her on a blanket and getting her to track bright toys. Yet even before she was three months old, the Ken-Crest staff had included in her May 15, 1974, activity sheet the following: "Hold her upright with her feet on the floor. Let go of your support *slightly* so she begins to bear weight on her feet." That activity astounded me initially but it was one more example of how Cara's program was broken down into tiny steps leading toward a sure, if distant, goal. Cara was already preparing for the day sixteen months later when she would take her first independent steps.

At the end of June, when she was four months old, Cara got her first report card, or in official Ken-Crest lingo, "teacher's progress report." It stated:

Cara has adjusted well to her new environment and has made considerable progress. Her gross motor development has been very good. She raises her head high when in a prone position and supports herself on her forearms for 30-second intervals. She rolls from supine to prone as well as from prone to supine spontaneously. She actively kicks and squirms on her tummy, moving herself forward short distances (4–6 inches). She lifts her extremities while on her stomach, so that she is in a U-shape, with only her stomach on the floor. She now turns her head to the right or left with no hesitation. She bears a fraction of weight on her legs. Her head control is improving; however, she exhibits some head bobbing when in a sitting position.

Cara reaches toward toys that are in her line of vision. She holds toys for brief periods. She clasps her hands together frequently. She visually tracks people as well as objects for short periods. She tracks toys and objects vertically and horizontally as well as circularly with little hesitation. She locates most voices and sounds with little difficulty. Cara vocalizes in response to others. Most of these sounds are musical cooings. Occasionally she vocalizes spontaneously to herself or others. Since Cara is breast-fed, there is little opportunity to observe her sucking or feeding behaviors. Cara is a lovable baby, who smiles, coos and occasionally squeals in delight. She enjoys physical contact and affection from adults. The awareness of being held is enough to calm her when she is crying.

As Cara grew a little older, she sometimes resisted certain activities introduced by the Ken-Crest staff. I, being soft-hearted, found it difficult to push her through an activity if she fussed or cried. Once again Mattie came to the rescue.

"When we'd introduce a new task, Cara would always be willing to try it. But after a few times, she'd resist if she didn't like it. It was usually with gross motor things, like getting her to hold a crawl position. Cara was never a long-term pouter. But if she pouted, it was a warning that, if you continue to do this, she'd burst into tears," Mattie said.

"Once I'd start to do something, I'd take a child through the whole process once so they would learn that crying would not stop the whole activity. If the task was hard and they cried, I'd always comfort them afterward, but I wouldn't make them repeat it right away. Things had to be forced on Cara to an extent, but all babies have a choice, or a choice should be offered. I always tell our staff that these children are people with emotions and we must respect them. 'Hey, you really are a person. You have a right to make choices.' Even if it's with a little baby, a choice can be offered between, say, a rattle and a ball."

I sometimes found it to be a delicate balance between offering Cara a choice of activities and getting her to follow through on an activity she didn't relish. One of Cara's least favorite tasks when she was about a year old was standing on her own feet. When Paul or I pulled her to a stand from a sitting position, Cara simply resisted by pulling up her legs, frog-style, and refusing to place her feet on the ground. It took a lot of our patience but she eventually stood.

Mattie and her staff lavished praise whenever a child accomplished a feat, no matter how small. The children picked up on this praise quickly and often applauded themselves or other children.

One morning early in his toilet training days, Mark was sitting on a potty chair off to the side of the room. No one was in the immediate vicinity to witness his great deed of peeing in the potty, so Mark toddled to the middle of the room, his pants dangling around his ankles, and applauded himself. When the staff realized Mark's message, they joined in the applause.

During Cara's first summer, when she was five months old, I introduced her to fruit juice from a cup. Until then her sole source of nourishment was breast milk. I never gave Cara a bottle because I not only hated the bother of bottles but saw no reason why she needed them. She got all the sucking and nutrition she needed from breast milk, so why, I reasoned, introduce a bottle which she'll only have to break away from eventually? Dr. Chandler supported me in this decision, and I never regretted it. She and David, who also never had a bottle, did not become thumbsuckers and both seem emotionally stable. Neither child really knew what to do with a bottle. As toddlers, when they saw another child's bottle, they would pick it up, look it over and try chewing on the nipple. "A curious object," read their facial expressions.

Soon after Cara began drinking liquids from a cup, I introduced her to simple solid foods. I began this about five or six months of age not because I felt she needed cereal or puréed fruit for nourishment—she was getting highest quality nourishment from breast milk—but because she

needed, as the Ken-Crest staff pointed out, the sensory experience of different tastes and textures. Such variety made Cara aware of her mouth. That awareness led to exploring the inside of her mouth with her tongue. All this was done not to make a gourmet of Cara but to prepare her for speech. The tongue must learn to take many positions within the mouth cavity to form sounds. With Cara and other Down's syndrome children the prerequisites to speech had to be taught early because fluid speech doesn't come as naturally to them as it does to other children.

One complication for Down's syndrome children is the proportion between the size of the tongue and the mouth cavity. Some say the tongue is too large, others that the mouth is too small. The result is the same: Down's children almost always let their tongues dangle out of their mouths. This tendency has been ignored by some parents to the point that the child plays with the tongue, pulls at it, sometimes even touches the chin with the tip of the tongue. This unattractive habit needn't develop if the child is trained young to keep the tongue within the mouth. Ken-Crest's staff used a variety of techniques to teach children to control their tongues. One of the most effective was to touch the tongue tip with an ice cube. The cold sensation caused the tongue to pull in quickly while the teacher simultaneously said, "Keep your tongue inside." Gradually use of the ice cube was diminished and the verbal reminder was enough.

Another technique was simply to touch the dangling tongue with the finger and remind the child to "keep it inside." But that trick didn't work with Cara. She thought it was fun to stick out her tongue and have the teacher touch it, and she would repeat the act to get the teacher to play her game. When the teachers caught on, they stopped the touching and only gave Cara verbal reminders. So much for that game. Tongue control became a habit for Cara by the time she was two or three. On the few occasions she did let her tongue droop—and it usually occurred when she was tired—a quiet verbal reminder was sufficient.

Different taste sensations also helped educate the tongue. A swab of peanut butter was a delightfully gooey way to show a baby that she had a roof to her mouth, and that, if the tongue reached up to that roof, it could taste the peanut butter placed there by an ingenious adult. Similarly the tongue was taught to move from side to side when dabs of jelly were placed on the inside of each cheek. Though these may sound like frivolous exercises, they were highly successful in teaching a lax tongue its way around the mouth. Such tasty explorations developed tongue control and mouth muscles necessary for speech later.

Chewing was equally important to speech development. But Cara was not fond of the effort of chewing, or so we thought. Cara came home from Ken-Crest just before noon, but the staff often offered her some of the hot lunch prepared for the older, all-day children. This food was presented as a chewing and swallowing exercise. Cara was unimpressed by Hazel Williams' cooking, particularly the meat, though everyone else thought Hazel rivaled Julia Child. But one day Hazel must have done something right by Cara, because her diaper bag brought home the following note from Sallie Robinson, an aide in Cara's class: "We offered Cara some lunch (fried fish, mixed vegetables, and noodles). She ate it very well. It was not mashed, only cut in bite-sized pieces. She didn't even spit any out! She is also using her lips and tongue to get crumbs into her mouth!! We were really pleased and knew you would be too!"

When I first offered Cara baby foods, both commercial ones and our leftovers puréed in the blender, she ate meats along with everything else. But as she grew and I gradually substituted cut-up pieces of adult food, she resisted all meats. Mattie and her staff thought Cara was lazy about chewing. "Yet I couldn't believe it when I saw her bite and chew an entire apple," said Sallie at the Ken-Crest Halloween party when Cara was twenty months old. And I couldn't believe it was laziness about chewing when I witnessed her laboriously chewing her way through hard, tough bagels. Cara seemed to go to any effort to chew something she really enjoyed. But she wouldn't give meat a chance. She cemented her lips together to prevent even a tiny piece from entering her mouth. I thought the smell of meat might have turned her off. I never forced her to eat meat, though I did try devious ways of slipping it to her, such as smearing a little between the bread and peanut butter in a sandwich. I often wondered, "Why am I doing this? Plenty of vegetarians survive quite nicely without meat." But somehow my maternal instincts commanded, "Get some meat into her." Meanwhile, I made certain she had plenty of protein from cheese, eggs, milk and natural peanut butter.

It wasn't until Cara was three that she discovered meat through, I'm ashamed to say, fast-food hamburgers. She began to eat fish about the same time when Bessie deLone, our next-door neighbor who is two years older than Cara, had dinner with us one night and ate fish. Inspired by Bessie, Cara then accepted fish as a regular staple of her diet. Soon followed all-beef and all-chicken hot dogs, lasagne with ground beef, and homemade hamburgers. When we visited my parents for Thanksgiving weekend, three months before she turned six, Cara ate turkey for the first time one night, lamb another night, and beef fondue another. But buttered rolls were the carrot on a stick—she couldn't have a roll until she ate so many bites of meat. Her queendom for a buttered roll.

Just as the goal of walking was broken down into tiny steps introduced long before Cara was ready to walk, so too were the goals of writing, zipping, buttoning, shoe buckling and tying, and other fine motor skills normally associated with children four to seven years of age. The key to these skills is good eye-hand coordination. And again, why not start building that coordination early? It began in infancy when Cara was given a variety of activities to develop awareness of her hands—having her wear the brightly colored mittens, encouraging her to reach for and grasp objects, rubbing her hands and fingers individually with the different textures of sandpaper, cotton, wood, stone, and water.

When she was able to sit alone, in a chair with a tray across it or at a table, Cara was given large pegs to remove from a board. The pegs first introduced were about an inch thick, just the right size for her tiny fist to hold comfortably. Later smaller pegs were offered. An infant's first method of picking up a small object like a peg is to palm it, scoop it up into the palm with all the fingers. As the child becomes more adroit, she learns to handle a small peg between the thumb and index finger. This is called the "inferior pincer" grip. This was quite difficult for Cara. Her less sophisticated method of picking up a small object was to use the middle finger and thumb. To correct this and to encourage the inferior pincer grip, an adult would gently hold a hand over hers to keep her three fingers curled under into her palm, leaving only the index finger and thumb free to work.

When Cara was eleven months old, her activity sheet suggested giving her fat marking pens: "Be sure she holds them in a fisted grasp and show her how to make random scribbles. Use large stacking rings and have Cara remove as many as possible. Do not allow her to put them in her mouth. Help her if necessary. Encourage her to pick up small edible objects (raisins, Froot Loops, Trix, pieces of cookie, etc.) using the inferior pincer." All these fine motor exercises paid off. By the time she was five, Cara held a pencil correctly and could print her name. Not well, but legibly. By that age she was also learning to buckle her shoes. I never envisioned her doing these skills when she was an infant placing stubby red pegs in the holes of a wooden block. But all those pegs, all those puzzles, all those millions of Cheerios picked up each morning, led to good small motor skills and eye-hand coordination years later.

As she neared her first birthday, Cara's progress astounded us. Paul and I recognized how much joy she had given us in that first year—a year that had begun in sudden, unexpected agony over her diagnosis, a year that was ending with the clear recognition that this little lady was a great treasure. She was a responsive, happy, smiling, laughing, creeping crawler who was giving us as much joy as any "normal" baby, perhaps even more because she was making far more physical and mental progress than we had expected.

At age one Cara was learning to stand up from a sitting position and to hold on to a table or chair and stand independently for a short while. If we held out a toy, she could be enticed to take a few steps while holding on to a secure chair or table. Before she tired of the standing position, she was shown how to get down in the proper sequence. It may be mind-boggling to an adult, but a baby just learning to stand sometimes needs to be shown how to sit down. If not, the result may be a hard landing. Cara and many of the other Ken-Crest babies needed to be shown how to get down to a half-kneel and then a side-sit.

Another of Cara's scholastic assignments was to increase her belly crawling distance. The difference between "creep" and "crawl" always stumped me. A crawl was just that—belly on floor, crawl along. A creep, however, was an up-on-hands-and-knees position. Cara had to be placed in that creep position and encouraged to creep along rather than flop down to the easier, more familiar crawl.

A category called "object relations" entered Cara's curriculum near the

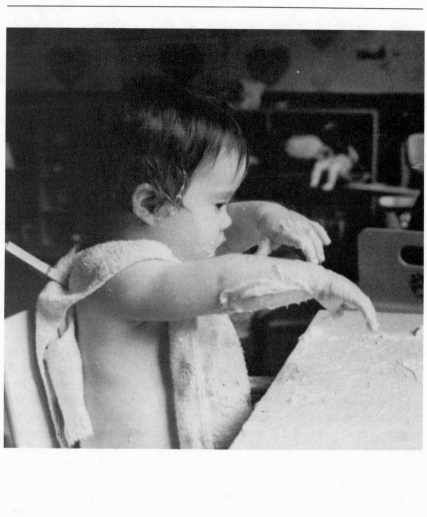

end of her first year. She began by visually tracking falling objects. Soon it rained plastic toys. By eleven months of age, she was "visually tracking the direction of fallen toys 50 percent of the time." (The Ken-Crest staff built into infants' goal sheets certain percentages of performance. No child was expected to perform a specific task 100 percent of the time for that task to be considered accomplished. Even babies were allowed to have bad days.)

"Object relations" also included activities such as hiding a small toy under a cloth and helping Cara to remove the covering. As she got the idea that she could recover the hidden toy by lifting off the cloth or hand-kerchief, she received less assistance. Small bits of food were also con-cealed under a cup for her to remove. Another way to show her how objects relate was to entice her to pull a string to move a desired toy closer.

When Cara was about six months old, I noticed that her vocalization, her cooing and gurgling, seemed to decrease. The Ken-Crest staff sug-gested that I leave Cara in one room and go to another to give her a quiet opportunity to vocalize on her own. That seemed to work. Her babbling increased. When she was eleven months old, Cara was imitating pat-a-cake 25 percent of the time, which had been a goal under the hearing and language category. Activities like showing her pictures or toys, singing to her, tickling her, or swinging her about with a "Wheeeee!" also invited her to respond vocally. The staff and Paul and I were very aware at this time of using Cara's name frequently because it was important that she respond to it. We encouraged her to play in front of a mirror so she would vocalize at her own image. We also gave her simple commands. For instance, we would give her a cube, allow her to play with it a short while and then ask her to "give me" while we put out a hand. We tried to keep these little orders short and direct and not to embroider them with verbiage.

Another goal at this stage was to get Cara to remove her socks while lying on her back. When this activity was introduced, an adult made it easier by pulling the sock over the heel, leaving Cara only the job of pull-ing the sock off from the toes. At first we showed her how by placing our hand over hers. This hand-over-hand introduction was used for many ac-tivities. Once Cara caught on, we dropped the assistance. Sock removal was the beginning of Cara's undressing career, but it also meshed with her language program because we always linked it with a verbal command, "Take your socks off, Cara." Sock removal soon became a favorite accomplishment and socks were whipped off in all kinds of weather. Putting them back on was another matter. But several months later I discovered Cara trying to pull on one of Paul's socks. Because it was so large for her tiny foot, the job was easy. I realized that she had taught me two things: that she was ready and interested in beginning to dress herself, and that using an oversized item made the job easier—it was a good way of building success into a new task. The incident opened my eyes to the fact that I should observe Cara more closely because she would undoubtedly teach me other lessons about when and how she was ready to learn something new.

As she entered the second year of her life, Cara was coming closer to walking. One of her thirteen-month-old tasks was to stand with her back to a wall for a minute, with no front support, once a day. This made her bear weight on her feet, familiarized her with an upright position, strengthened her legs and back, and helped her develop the balance necessary for walking. A similar prerequisite-to-walking activity at this age was to get Cara to move from a squat to a stand while she was supported at the hips. Her goal sheet suggested this be done twice a day and that she be rewarded with a Froot Loop.

When I learned that the Ken-Crest staff sometimes used M-and-M's candy as a reward, I questioned the practice. I didn't agree with giving candy as a reward and I also had some hesitancy about the whole behavior modification business of bribing with food. Mattie explained that M-and-M's were used only rarely and that they would never be given to Cara if I so desired. She explained that the general philosophy was to use raisins, Froot Loops, bits of cookie or whatever, only when a task was introduced, and to replace the food gradually with verbal praise and applause. That satisfied me. But there were no more M-and-M's for Cara.

"Cara's gross motor continues to improve," her home visit report noted when she was fourteen months old. "She stands and steps well for her mother. She pulled up to a stand several times while we were there." Over the next few spring and summer months, Cara stood unsupported for increased time spans. And she discovered "cruising," side-stepping her way around tables, sofas, or anything about eighteen inches off the floor, while holding on to the handy object. Several times it seemed she was on the brink of letting go and taking a first independent step. This "almost ready" stage seemed to linger and I began to wonder when she would actually walk alone. She seemed to be spending too long in the cruising period, my impatience told me. But in August we spent two weeks at a South Carolina beach with two families we knew and loved from our days in the South. Both families had two children each. Betsy and Will Ray were then five and three. Evan Covington was four and her little brother Owen had just turned one. Though Cara was five months older than Owen, they were about the same size. Owen had just started walking and was into everything. He particularly enjoyed climbing on chairs, which would then topple backwards. Owen and Cara quickly became pals. Cara enjoyed cruising around in pursuit of Owen who was thoroughly enjoying his new-found freedom of walking. Perhaps peer pressure doesn't exist among one-year-olds, but Owen clearly showed Cara that walking could be terrific. Four days after we returned home from vacation, Cara walked alone for the first time.

At age one, Cara's receptive language was blossoming. She understood simple commands and, being one who likes to please, she readily responded. She began to learn the names of the parts of her body and could, when asked, point to her toes and tummy when she was fifteen months old. In giving her directions at this age, we tried to be specific: "Please give me your blue shirt" was better than "Get that shirt, please." (Which shirt?) Simple verbal requests made without pointing to "this" or "that" and without looking in the direction of the item made Cara rely solely on the spoken word. There were times, of course, when a clue was needed. But we tried to use one only when she did not understand the spoken word.

Between eighteen months and her second birthday, Cara whisked through a number of achievements: spoon feeding herself, learning the differences between "on" and "in," "under" and "over," building towers of four or five blocks, pointing to her mouth, eyes, hair, hands, ear, head, legs, arms, front, back and sides when asked, pointing to her own property, matching "big" versus "little" objects or people, repeating tapped rhythms, and stringing large beads.

This period also ushered in an achievement dear to every parent's heart—toilet training. I was pregnant and expecting David in February 1976, just before Cara's second birthday. Paul and I thought it might be smart to begin Cara's toilet training before we became busy with a new infant. So, three months before the new baby was expected, I asked Mattie about toilet training. "When will she be ready?" I asked. "When you are," Mattie replied. "You've got to be ready because it will take a lot of work and time."

We began then, when Cara was twenty-one months old, by checking her diaper regularly and noting on a chart the times she was dry, wet, or had moved her bowels. Once we recognized her patterns—that she was wet between 8:30 and 9:00 A.M. nearly every day, for instance—we began by sitting her on the potty chair a few minutes before we anticipated she would urinate or move her bowels.

Cara became "scheduled trained" within about six months; that is, she would stay dry between times we took her to the potty, although she did not initiate these potty trips until she was nearly four. She is blessed with an iron bladder and needed only to be reminded to go to the potty every four hours or so. From the time she was two-and-a-half until she was five, she wore diapers only at night. When we bought the last box of overnight Pampers when she was five, we had to take her to the toilet about midnight. A full bladder tended to wake her up, so taking her again at four or five helped her to sleep later than six in the morning. That seems terribly burdensome to the childless, but it wasn't all that difficult. Usually Paul or I awoke at some point anyway and, by taking both Cara and David, I had less laundry to do.

In Cara's first year she was fed, kept warm and clean, played with, talked to and loved. She was stimulated by an abundance of toys and activities both at home and at school. In a sense she hadn't a care in the world. But in fact Cara had already begun to learn to concentrate, to work hard, and to recognize limits.

After her first birthday, suddenly there were many things she could not do—such as bite Mommy or Daddy. When I told the Ken-Crest staff that

Cara was developing this biting habit, they suggested that I simply say, "Stop," in place of the negative command, "Don't bite." Though I was unaware of it when Cara was only one, this technique laid the groundwork for the same kind of positive discipline she would encounter later in her Montessori school, where children were told, for instance, "walk" rather than "don't run" in the hallways.

I knew that at about age one most babies begin to need limits. Several years before Cara was born I interviewed Dr. Mary Ainsworth, a psychologist then at Johns Hopkins University, about her nine-year research project on mother-infant relationships. She had made detailed studies of twenty-six Baltimore babies—when they cried, how often they cried, who picked them up, how long they were held, and a myriad of other details of their daily lives. One of Dr. Ainsworth's conclusions was that babies who were picked up quickly and comforted for a healthy length of time tended to diminish their fussing and eventually fussed less often. Some people might say that Dr. Ainsworth was advocating spoiling the child, but her findings showed that this apparent "spoiling" resulted in happier, less clingy children.

Dictating orders or physically interfering with the actions of a baby under a year of age usually are unproductive when trying to change a baby's behavior, Dr. Ainsworth found. "In fact there was a negative correlation between infant compliance and the number of commands a mother issued or the extent to which she physically interfered to reinforce her commands," Dr. Ainsworth said. "But there's a point at the beginning of the second year when this has to change. The first year they have confidence that they're controlling things. But you can't go through life that way." As Cara began her second year, I recalled Dr. Ainsworth's advice. And it conveniently meshed with the philosophy the Ken-Crest staff held about setting limits for a young child.

Increasing Cara's attention span and concentration powers was another goal of Cara's second year. One of the goals set forth in her April 1975 goal sheet was "Cara will attend to an activity for thirty seconds without supervision once each day. She will receive applause and verbal praise." Another was "Cara will push a toy five inches while sitting at the toddler table twice a day. She will receive praise and affection." Her June report card noted "Cara is now playing with stacking cups. She seems to have more control putting pegs in a board." It suggested that we "increase Cara's attention span by making her play with one toy at a time."

These quiet activities, done one at a time at a table or high chair, isolated a task without distractions. This method helped her perform the task, such as putting pegs in a board, more successfully and initiated a pattern of learning which she carries with her to this day. When I watch her now, at age eight, pull several books from the shelf, line them up on the big pillow in the playroom and read each one from cover to cover, I realize how her early experiences fostered this ability to concentrate. And she has taught me not to interrupt her concentrated work. If I remind her that it is time for dinner or time for school, she will politely but firmly tell me, "Not until I finish reading."

FIVE

"Early One Bright Morning a Small Fuzzy Duckling Went for a Walk"

Cara's second birthday marked another major change in our lives—namely, a lively, demanding little sibling named David Harry Jablow, born eight days before Cara's second birthday. Paul and I wanted Cara to have a brother or sister, one who was healthy and normal. When I knew I was pregnant in July 1975, I felt sure that this child would be all right. I simply could not believe this child would also be retarded or handicapped in any way. Perhaps I was daring fate, but I truly believed that. The more skeptical Paul thought our chances of a normal baby were probably good. But we both knew that fate changes the statistics as a woman grows older. I had crossed the line—I was thirty when David was conceived. Women under thirty have a 1-in-1500 chance of bearing a Down's syndrome child; women thirty to thirty-four, a 1-in-750 chance; women thirty-five to thirty-nine, a 1-in-280 chance; women forty to forty-four, a 1-in-130 chance; and women forty-five and older, a 1-in-65 chance. There was also a recurrence factor: once a woman under thirty has a Down's child, her chances of a repeat increase 1 or 2 percent.

One comfort to women over thirty is a relatively new procedure called amniocentesis. A physician inserts a needle through the abdominal wall and into the uterus of a woman at least fifteen weeks pregnant and withdraws a small amount of amniotic fluid. This amniotic fluid contains enough discarded fetal cells for a laboratory to determine a great deal of information about the unborn infant, including the child's sex and a number of chromosomal conditions such as whether or not the child has Down's syndrome or will be born with Tay-Sachs disease.

When I knew I was pregnant, we told our immediate families but didn't broadcast the news until after the amniocentesis results. And therein lay a dilemma. What if the amniocentesis showed that this new child had Down's syndrome too? Would we, could we, raise another? I was afraid if we had a repeat performance, it would crush Paul. As much as he loves Cara, he badly wanted a normal child. For him, the answer would be obvious: abortion.

It wasn't that easy for me. I grew up in the fold of the Roman Catholic Church. Though I could intellectually support abortion as another woman's right, I could not bring myself to support it personally on the emotional level. It was—that little Catholic whisper kept filling my ear—another life, after all. This child had been conceived. It was planned and wanted. Its heart was beating inside me. I could hear that heartbeat on a stethoscope.

One side of me argued, "What if someone had told you, when you were pregnant with Cara, that she would be retarded. Would you have aborted her?" Of course not. But Paul's response to that argument was, "But you didn't know then that she was Cara. She wasn't a person to you before she was born."

Another side of me argued, "If this second child is also to be retarded, you must have an abortion. You can't make Paul and everyone else go through this again. Swallow the guilt, Martha, and do it if you have to." But I knew that, if I bought this argument, I could never accept the guilt. I might have concealed it, but it would be stuck in my throat for the rest of my life.

Opposing arguments tugged at me from the moment I knew I was pregnant until the amniocentesis results were in. But I never truly plunked my money down on either side. I knew—I just knew—this baby was all right, and that I'd never have to make that wretched decision.

Paul raised a question for the future, a rhetorical question, I felt. How would this child react to the fact that, if it had been known to be re-tarded, it might have been aborted? Paul felt we would have to answer that by saying, "If amniocentesis had shown you to be retarded and you had been aborted, you wouldn't have been the same person you are to-day." To me, that was a remote situation which I spent little time ponder-ing. But it was a serious concern of Paul's.

When Dr. Franklin and I discussed amniocentesis, he advised waiting a few weeks beyond the fifteenth-week-of-pregnancy minimum. An extra week or two gave the fetus more time to mature and gave the test a bet-ter chance of accuracy, he said. He scheduled the amniocentesis for an October Friday at Jefferson. I arranged for Cara to stay at Ken-Crest longer than usual that day and drove into center city where I met Paul at Jefferson. The place was institutionally bleak with its gray walls and tile. The atmosphere was hardly conducive to easing one's tension. Dr. Frank-lin had explained the procedure clearly and I had faith in his skill, yet I was still tense about having a needle poked into my belly. A few minutes after Dr. Franklin stepped off the elevator, we were ushered into a small room by a cheery, plump nurse. Dr. Franklin shed the jacket of his three-piece suit for a hospital gown and gloves. Paul was allowed to stay in the room to watch. The whole procedure was very informal. As I reclined on the bed, Dr. Franklin unwrapped a sterile amniocentesis kit. It was a dif-ferent model than those he'd previously used and he joked about having to read the directions. With slight pressure, he put his hand over my belly to feel the position of the fetus.

"It's like the last olive left in the bottle," he said. "There's plenty of room for the fetus to bob around." He gave me a local anesthetic and inserted the needle. I lifted my head to watch the almost clear liquid slowly fill the small vial of the needle to the 20-cc mark, about two-thirds of an ounce. No more difficult than giving a blood sample, I thought. But it seemed to my non-medical mind that he was extracting a lot of fluid from my still small uterus.

"Are you going to leave enough for the baby to swim around in?" I asked Dr. Franklin.

"Oh, yes. There's plenty left."

Twenty minutes after we entered the room, the whole thing was over. "I'll take this over to the lab myself," Dr. Franklin said as he capped the vial. "Don't worry about this one."

I thanked him and I felt he was right—I didn't have to worry about this one. But it would be pleasant to ride out the rest of the pregnancy free of this worry. Paul went back to work and I drove to Ken-Crest to pick up Cara. Now the three-to-four-week wait for the lab results began.

After three weeks of silence from the Jefferson lab, I called Dr. Franklin's office. His nurse said he hadn't heard from Jefferson either but would look into it. When we hadn't heard anything by the end of the next week, I called Dr. Franklin again. If the news was bad, I needed to know soon. The further into the pregnancy, the more complicated an abortion could be. For the first time since I'd met him, Dr. Franklin revealed abruptness and impatience. "My calling them again won't hurry the lab work," he said rather curtly. I thought he might have had a rough day, or been up all night delivering babies. Obstetricians are entitled to a little impatience, I supposed. Yet I was hurt and angry at his response.

He called a few days later. "Good news," he said. "Nothing to worry about now."

"That's terrific," I said, "But what took them so long?"

"I guess they were doing some research work with the sample," he replied.

"Damn them," I thought, for playing research games with my amniotic fluid and my emotions. If the sample had shown an extra chromosome, would they have told us sooner? Well, that was all moot now.

"Oh, one other thing, Dr. Franklin. Is it a boy or girl?"

"Do you really want to know?" he asked.

"Of course I want to know."

"Well, think it over. Wouldn't you like to learn the way parents usually do, at the time of birth?"

"No, I'd like to know now."

"I like to discourage parents from learning the baby's sex before it's born because they may put a lot of importance on the child's sex and, if the test turns out to be wrong . . ."

"Wrong?"

"Well, yes, that happened once several years ago. We thought it was going to be a boy and it turned out to be a girl. Luckily in that case, the parents weren't disappointed, though."

"It's not important to us, whether it's a boy or girl. We'll be happy with either as long as it's healthy," I insisted.

"Okay, but talk it over with your husband, will you? And consider the possibility of keeping it a mystery until the baby's born."

Paul and I did weigh Dr. Franklin's remarks. But neither of us—perhaps because we were reporters—could tolerate the idea of someone's knowing a fact and not sharing it with us, especially when it was *our* fact.

Paul called Dr. Franklin back the next day and told him that we had talked it over, and that we wouldn't be disappointed either way. And we really wanted to know.

"All right. Your child is male," Dr. Franklin said.

I proceeded to buy blue and white wallpaper and make blue and white striped curtains for "his" room. If the Jefferson lab people were wrong, I'd invite them to come out to the house and strip off the blue and white wallpaper.

When I had amniocentesis in 1975, it was performed only at a limited number of major medical centers. It is performed more often each year and with greater sophistication—namely, the use of ultrasound to monitor the fetus's location and position. As contemporary as ultrasound and amniocentesis may sound, their days may be numbered. As Cara was turning five and David three, a Stanford University research team was discovering that cells from a fetus appear in its mother's blood stream as early as the twelfth week of pregnancy. The next step is to develop a blood test which could be used on all women early in pregnancy. This would eliminate the slight risk involved in amniocentesis and the complex lab work that accompanies it. But Dr. Leonard A. Herzenberg, head of the Stanford team, has said it will take years to develop a blood test for Down's syndrome.

Selecting a name was no problem once we knew that "he" would be a "he." Before Cara was born, I had chosen several girl's names and Paul had selected a boy's name. We didn't intend our choices to be along strict sex lines—it just happened that way. I found it difficult to choose among my top three or four female names. But Paul had a clear favorite in the male category: David. That was fine with me because my grandfather's name had been David. Paul selected Harry as David's middle name in honor of his late father.

"Oh, I see you're going to have a boy," remarked a Booth midwife as she looked over my medical folder during a prenatal check-up a few months before David was born. The folder contained David's karyotype, the blown-up photograph of his chromosomes, the hard, black-and-white evidence that he was a boy and that he had no chromosomal abnormalities.

I was fascinated by this genetic roadmap of the child I was carrying. It was an amazing and eerie phenomenon to know this child inside me was a boy, that he was "David" even before he was born. Most pregnant women and their husbands refer to their child as "it" or "the baby" in a rather impersonal way before birth. Yet Paul and I talked of David as if we had already met him.

And we did meet him on February 19, 1976, at 8:15 A.M. I awoke early that morning and realized that it was time to get to Booth. We'd previously arranged with our friends the Maidenbergs to drop Cara at their house on the way to Booth, even if it was in the middle of the night. Mike Maidenberg groggily answered the phone when I called at 5 A.M., "Okay, bring her over."

We snatched Cara from her crib and bundled her in a heavy blanket. Kitty Maidenberg, as wide awake as she'd be at noon, had her porch light on and met us at the door. Paul started talking to Kitty about something unimportant—what Cara would eat for breakfast or whatever—but I was in a hurry. "Come on, let's go," I snapped. "Kitty knows what to do."

David's delivery was much like Cara's but swifter. I was panting my Lamaze exercises at 7:00 A.M. when the Booth nurses were bringing around breakfast. I was in no state to look at food. But Paul was taking this second birth like a veteran. "Would you like something to eat, Mr. Jablow?" one of the nurses asked. "Sure, thank you," he said at the moment the midwife attending me decided it was time to move me from the labor room into the adjacent delivery room. I was ready and anxious to get moving but Paul seemed wrapped up in his danish and coffee. He wolfed them down while helping to roll my bed into the delivery room. I was furious with him for his relaxed attention to food while I was having strong contractions. But short temper is a natural characteristic of the transition stage of labor, which I was in at that moment.

David weighed in at six pounds, eleven ounces. The umbilical cord was wrapped around his neck not once but twice. As soon as the midwife saw this she snatched a scissors and cut the cord. She later remarked, "That was some cord. I've never seen one that strong and flexible."

I later recalled the incident with some humor because a month earlier, when I was wallpapering David's room, my mother had warned me, "I wish you wouldn't do that wallpapering, Martha. You know, Nana Moraghan [my father's mother] would have said that reaching up to hang that paper will cause the cord to wrap around the baby's neck."

I laughed off Mom's warning at the time, but as David's personality has evolved over his first few years, I have seen a lot of similarities between him and Nana Moraghan. Perhaps they were in cahoots over the cord incident all along.

Paul was thrilled to have a son. He idolized his own father who had died when Paul was twelve. Paul cherished the father-son relationship and looked forward to the day when he and David could go places and do things together—namely, go to the ball park and eat hot dogs.

Paul held David minutes after he was born. We spent the next several hours getting acquainted with David back in room 235, the same room Cara and I had occupied two years earlier. I was famished after the exhaustion of labor and delivery and I devoured the breakfast I was denied earlier when Paul had his coffee and danish. While I ate, Paul held David in his green-hospital-gowned arms. It was such a happy scene in contrast to the tense drama played out in the same room two years earlier.

About noon Paul left Booth to pick up Cara at the Maidenbergs. He found her playing happily and wearing Teddy's clothes because we had forgotten to bring along her own things in our hasty 5:00 A.M. exit. Kitty asked Paul to have some lunch. "Oh, no, I can't, thanks," he said. But Kitty exerted only a little pressure, she later enjoyed retelling, and Paul was soon consuming two salami sandwiches washed down with three Rolling

Rock beers. Kitty was amused to see the sandwiches and beer drain away Paul's tension of the morning.

Paul had called my mother from Booth while I was in labor. She caught a train from New Haven and was in Philadelphia by mid-afternoon. She and Cara had a fine time together while David and I stayed at Booth for three days. David was to be released Sunday morning. One of the nurses had remarked that he looked a little jaundiced. I thought he looked a bit yellow, too, but I didn't want to admit it. Paul arrived Sunday morning to bring us home, and we waited anxiously for the pediatrician on duty to give David his final exam and freedom papers. No one seemed to know what was delaying the doctor and the longer we waited, the more anxious I grew. Finally he came by our room to look at David. If he says he's jaundiced and can't go home, I'll kick him and take David home anyway, I thought. I was not going to repeat the same script we'd had with Cara. But the young pediatrician said he thought the jaundice was so slight that it would be all right to take him home. Bless you, you don't know what an argument you've just avoided, I thought.

Taking David home was a joy, heightened I'm sure by the contrast to Cara's homecoming. An added bonus was the presence of Kathleen Sullivan. She had been in Atlantic City to speak to a group of school principals and had come through Philadelphia to visit us. She and my mother remarked about what a happy contrast this day was to their visits two years earlier.

We had tried to prepare Cara for the arrival of a little brother by talking to her about a "baby coming." Several weeks before, I had bought her a book about babies with wonderful illustrations of an older sister cuddling a new baby. She loved the book and wanted it read and reread. But when we brought David home, she virtually ignored him. She was delighted to see me again, but David was only a momentary curiosity.

Over the next several months I was often asked how Cara was taking to David—"Any sibling rivalry?" But she took him in stride and showed hardly any jealousy. Occasionally she wanted to sit in my lap when I was nursing David. I asked her instead to get a book, and she sat next to me with my arm around her while I read her a story. This seemed to satisfy her.

It was also a time when books became a major interest in her young life. One favorite was "The Fuzzy Duckling,"* which I remember my brother's having when he was young. I remember it distinctly because Mike's remark about one particular illustration has been repeated often by our family to document his insight and my personality. He is reported to have said, as he pointed to the one black sheep on a page of white ones, "That's Marth." He couldn't have known the connotation of a black sheep when he was three years old. I thought he saw the similarity between the sheep's dark fleece and my dark hair. But everyone else in my family said his remark showed his brilliant perception of my personality.

Cara liked "The Fuzzy Duckling," I think, because of its warm illustrations and the rhythmic repetition of the story. With each of the seven types of animals the duckling meets, he asks, "Will you come for a walk with me?" On the nth reading of the story, I paused unintentionally and Cara piped up with the next word. I realized she had the story down pat, so I began a little game of purposely leaving a phrase hanging. She always filled in the correct word:

Me: "Early one bright . . ."
Cara: "morning . . ."
Me: "a small fuzzy duckling went for a . . ."
Cara: "walk."

She loved participating in the story. I began playing the same game with other familiar books. On the next home visit from the Ken-Crest staff, we pulled out "The Fuzzy Duckling" to show off. Nancy Nowell and Mattie were flabbergasted. Cara was flooded with praise and she beamed back her pride.

I have saved that book. I've taped the worn binding and its one torn page. I cut off the top right corner which had been chewed by either David or Cara—both went through stages of literally devouring books. I'm preserving that book because it marks the beginning of Cara's remarkable reading career. No one expected her to start sounding out words phonetically when she was four or to read smoothly when she was five. Certainly she didn't "read" "The Fuzzy Duckling" when she was two, but I think that was the beginning of her reading.

*Written by Jane Werner, illustrated by Alice and Martin Provensen (Racine, Wisconsin: Golden Press, 1974).

Speech and language were being heavily emphasized by the Ken-Crest staff as Cara turned two. Her receptive language was good: she understood directions such as "put the ball on the table"; "look up at the light"; "look down at your toes." She knew she was a "gurl," as she said, and David was a boy. At eighteen months, Cara was evaluated by a Ken-Crest speech pathologist, who found that her receptive language age was fourteen months and her expressive language age was twelve months.

Around this time Mattie attended a special workshop about language development in delayed children. She came back eager to apply some new approaches to Cara. Mattie wrote out eleven exercises that she used at Ken-Crest for us to use at home: encourage Cara to place her tongue to the roof of her mouth and make an *l* sound; encourage her to move her tongue from side to side and up and down outside the mouth; encourage her to do a biting motion; encourage her to twist her mouth from side to side; encourage her to imitate vowel sounds and use exaggerated mouth formations in showing her; encourage her to imitate isolated consonant sounds starting with *d*, *b*, *m* and *n*; encourage her to imitate combinations of consonant and vowel using the same beginning consonants such as *da*, *de*, *di*, *do*; continue to read and sing to Cara; continue to use the proper names for toys, objects and food; give her lots of opportunities to verbalize her desires and try to ignore her gestures when she wants something; give her simple commands such as naming parts of the body and articles of clothing.

And, Mattie noted, "The speech pathologist recommends that Cara be given regular table food and pieces of meat so that her bite, chewing and swallowing sequence will become more sophisticated. All three areas are very important when developing good speech patterns."

When Mattie tried all these "encourage her to's" at Ken-Crest, she took Cara out of the classroom to a quiet corner of the building. Cara sat in Mattie's lap as they faced a mirror and named animals from picture cards or made consonant and vowel sounds. Mattie spent ten to twenty minutes each day in front of the mirror with Cara. We felt very fortunate that the class was small enough that Mattie could afford to lavish this much individual attention on Cara.

It was about this age, too, that Cara began watching "Sesame Street." Its concentration on letters and sounds, like Cara's interest in her alphabet wallpaper and her school work with Mattie, increased her language skills. By age two and a half, she could identify and name each letter and recite the whole alphabet from memory.

But language wasn't her only course of study at this age. There were many discoveries to be made and skills to be acquired. It wasn't always easy or quick with Cara. New skills don't come as spontaneously to her as to most children. She had to learn to pull up her underpants first and then her overalls each time she got up from the potty, for instance. A child like David needed only to be told once or twice and that became a habit. But Cara needed constant help and reminding for months before she habitually pulled up her clothing correctly. Her pace was like a slow-motion movie. It required patience but she gave back such love and such pride in her own accomplishments that the price of patience was small. And the reward was in hearing her say, with each effort, "I do it myself." Holding back assistance took much more time, but it fostered her independence. There must have been a million times when I have wanted to hurry Cara along by zipping her jacket or buckling her shoes, but I try to hold back. I don't want to crush her desire to do what she can for herself.

Cara became more social after her second birthday. She became more aware of the other children in the Ken-Crest program. When Donald, one of the youngest babies, would cry, Cara would pat him. Or when Damont fussed, she would bring him a toy. Her empathy extended to the point of a quivering lower lip when another child was hurt or cried. She would break into tears if she weren't quickly told, "It's all right. He'll be all right. He'll stop crying."

In the spring after David was born and Cara turned two, Paul learned that he had won a fellowship to study at Stanford University under the National Endowment for the Humanities' program for journalists. It was to be a nine-month sabbatical to pursue any field of the humanities he wished, by taking non-credit courses, which meant there would be no exams or papers to write.

Paul was concerned that the move might interrupt Cara's progress. But we knew she couldn't stay at Ken-Crest forever for a number of reasons. Ken-Crest's funding specifications seemed to be in an annual bureaucratic turmoil. When Cara enrolled, the program was free and funded under Title IV-A.* That funding soon came under another federal title and by Cara's second year in the program, middle-income families were required to pay a small fee based on a sliding scale according to their income. We paid $19 a week. By the time Paul learned he'd won the Stanford fellowship, the funding regulations had changed again, and Cara faced ineligibility because we earned a few thousand dollars more a year than Title XX allowed. The Ken-Crest front office went to bat for us with the state bureaucrats because Ken-Crest felt a moral obligation to continue serving clients like Cara, since their service depended on the child's need, not the parents' income. But we knew that, even though there were bureaucratic routes of appeal, we would eventually lose. The rules, after all, were written by the very bureaucrats who would determine any appeal.

The move to California made all that moot. Even if we had not gone to California, Cara's strong progress seemed to point toward "mainstreaming," that is, placing her among "normal" nursery school children. Before Paul heard about the fellowship, I had investigated a Montessori school nearby with the idea that Cara might soon attend there. I had read about Montessori schools and was impressed with their emphasis on helping a child develop according to his or her individual needs and pace. Then I read Dr. Maria Montessori's "The Secret of Childhood" and was even more impressed with the respect and dignity with which Montessori children are regarded. A Montessori classroom seemed a natural successor to Cara's Ken-Crest program. I visited the Montessori school and observed a classroom one morning before we went to California. The headmistress was quite open to the idea of mainstreaming. She told me of another Down's syndrome child who had been through the same school until she was thirteen. I stored away that encouraging visit in my memory and hoped that Cara could enroll there when we returned from California.

In August 1976 we rented our house and prepared for the Pacific Coast. On Cara's last day at Ken-Crest, Mattie took her out of the room for

* Title IV-A of the Social Security Act of 1947 funded many social service programs, including special needs daycare. Title IV-A was replaced in 1975 by Title XX of the same act. Many Title IV-A programs were spun off from direct federal funding to Title XX, which channeled federal funds through state administrations.

a private goodbye. There were tears in Mattie's eyes and mine when they returned. Cara didn't understand the significance of this farewell, of course, but the most important chapter of her life was ending. She had spent nearly five hundred mornings in Mattie's loving care. But if a time to leave had to come, this one was appropriate. Mattie had just learned she was about to be promoted. She would soon be in charge of curriculum for several Ken-Crest centers and no longer a classroom teacher.

Cara's final Ken-Crest report was prepared for whoever would be her teacher in California:

At the time of separation from our program, Cara was functioning at the following levels:
Self-help skills: *Cara is schedule trained for a potty. She can undress herself with the exception of untying her shoes and unbuttoning. She can put her shoes and socks on from the toes and put on front-opened clothing with minimum assistance. She cannot put on pullover clothing, but can pull pants up from the floor to her waist. She feeds herself independently with a spoon, but is very selective in what foods she will eat. Our program included use of a variety of foods, emphasizing those requiring chewing or with unfamiliar textures.*
Fine motor skills: *Cara is able to complete simple puzzles, string large beads and screw and unscrew lids. She is able to build a tower of ten cubes and uses the pincer grasp to place small pegs in a board.*
Gross motor skills: *Cara can walk up and down stairs, using a handrail, although she prefers to crawl when allowed. She can throw a large ball and kick a large stationary ball. Her balance is good and she has been working on climbing a ladder and jumping with both feet off the ground.*
Self-image/cognitive skills: *Cara plays cooperatively with other children, taking turns, and engages in "pretend play." She knows her own name and the full names of all immediate family members. She is able to touch 25 body parts, on request, on herself or another person and recognizes herself in a picture. She distinguishes between big and little objects, and places objects up, down, in, on and out. She is working on over, under. She touches back and front on request. She is*

able to follow one-step verbal commands. Cara is able to attend to easy tasks for 10 minutes when supervised and to difficult tasks for five minutes when supervised.

Speech: *Cara keeps her tongue predominantly in her mouth although she does not keep her mouth closed except during eating and speech. She is unable to hold her mouth closed for more than 15 seconds and continue normal breathing patterns. We have been encouraging her to hold her mouth closed in a casual manner rather than making it a priority at this time. Her speech work centers around lip and tongue movements, picture recognition and blowing.*

Cara has no known allergies or health problems. Her parents are active and concerned and have been involved in all areas of our program. They should be considered a valuable resource for anyone working with Cara. Our main areas of concern at this time are Cara's speech and her eating habits. Occasionally, Cara gets "locked in" to whatever she is doing at the moment and refuses to move to a new task or follow a direction on her own. We have found that leading Cara through the change or first steps of the direction in a matter-of-fact manner gets willing cooperation on these few occasions.

With Cara's "graduation" from Ken-Crest, we packed a few clothes and toys and headed West.

SIX

"Cara Ate Lots of Loquats"

The vision of driving across country with a six-month-old and a two-and-a-half-year-old did not thrill Paul or me. "Maybe when they're older . . ." We took the battery out of the car, removed the tires, and left the car on cinderblocks next to my Uncle Bill's barn. We bought plane tickets to California. Like a nineteenth-century pioneer father, Paul went West ahead of the children and me to settle on housing, receive parcels shipped ahead, and buy a second-hand car.

Paul had succeeded in persuading the Stanford housing people to reassign us from a two-bedroom to a three-bedroom apartment, a change well worth the extra dollars, given Cara and David's different sleeping patterns. But the reassigned apartment had roaches, so Paul had to repack everything he had just unpacked while the place was sprayed. He spent the rest of the week wrangling with United Parcel Service about some mislaid packages which contained his most cherished, and irreplaceable, jazz records. When they were finally delivered safely we laughed at the discovery that the only material goods Paul really cared about were his records.

My move was not much smoother. For David the airline gave me an "air cradle," a wonderful euphemism for a cardboard box with a blanket folded in the bottom. David fell asleep immediately, however, and I envisioned a peaceful six-hour flight to the West Coast. No sooner were we airborne than the pilot's voice shattered the silence, waking David, to announce that we had some sort of mechanical problem that required a brief unscheduled stop. That stop, plus the scheduled one in Chicago, meant that David never went back to sleep. Cara dozed occasionally in the seat next to me. But the most annoying aspect of the flight was the laziness of the flight attendants. Never once did one offer any extra help to this poor woman traveling alone with an infant and a toddler. ("Wait until they have children of their own," I thought.) Somewhere over the Rockies, I had to flag one down to watch the children so I could go to the rest room.

Our initial experiences were not prophetic of the rest of the Stanford year. When the screen door swung shut as I entered the tiny apartment for the first time, I knew we were in for a nine-month vacation. The material concerns of our lives (calling the plumber, painting the living room) would be scaled down. I could stretch back and watch the children grow in the mild, northern California sun, Paul could relax from work pressures in the seminars for the Journalism Fellows and on the tennis court, and we could both audit courses.

Our apartment was in a cluster of two-story apartments for married students with children. In the center of each cluster was a play area of swings, sand piles and climbing equipment, an area almost never empty of barefooted children. Cara took to it immediately. Our apartment opened onto a patio and, beyond, a grassy area leading to the playground. But our quarters were tiny and confining in comparison to our spacious, high-ceilinged house in Philadelphia. We often escaped claustrophobia by taking jaunts into San Francisco for the day, or to the Napa Valley, Big Sur, the Redwood country as far as Eureka to the north and San Simeon to the south for a weekend. Paul and I knew we'd probably never have an opportunity like this again so we made the most of it. Cara and David were fine travelers, with the one exception of a Saturday night in the Napa Valley when David stayed awake all night. Every grape in the valley must have shivered on its vine from his howling that night.

A high priority after unpacking was to find a school for Cara. We had done a bit of preliminary scouting before flying to California by writing letters and asking questions of Stanford people. When we arrived, we narrowed the choices to three: a Montessori school, an infant-toddler program similar to Ken-Crest's, and Bing Nursery School, the on-campus Stanford nursery school where practice teaching and child-related research was done.

I was predisposed to the Montessori school because of my Montessori

reading and the positive impressions of the Montessori school I had visited in Philadelphia. But I soon learned that not all Montessori schools are alike. The one we visited in California seemed rigid. During our observation the children were serving each other a snack. All the children had to sit at the same time, silently, with their napkins in their laps, before the snack and juice could be distributed. One lively child put his napkin on his head and was politely but firmly reminded that his behavior was holding up all the other children's snacks. I thought this routine was a bit stiff for active preschoolers. But more than its inflexibility and lack of warmth between children and teachers, this particular school was quickly struck from our list for a specific reason. The teacher Cara would have had was a beautiful woman from Sri Lanka who was a well-trained and experienced Montessori teacher. Her speech was grammatically perfect but so heavily accented that it was difficult for Paul and me to understand her. We thought that speech was such a high priority for Cara at this point in her development that she needed the clearest adult model.

Next on our list was a program for retarded infants and toddlers. The class was small, held in a spacious, sunny room full of fine equipment and toys, and the teachers seemed as competent as any at Ken-Crest. As we observed the class, Cara plunged right into the classroom activity. A mother of one of the children in the class was also observing and asked us how old Cara was. Paul suggested that the woman ask Cara herself. She did and Cara put up two fingers and said, "Two." The mother seemed amazed, but Paul couldn't understand why.

The head teacher, Romaine Sternad, watched Cara moving right into the stream of classroom activity and concluded, "We would love to have Cara in our program. We have room for her and I know she'd fit right in. But she would be at the top of the class both in age and ability and I'm not sure that's what would be best for her. She really should have models above her functioning levels to challenge her and to socialize with." We could not disagree.

When we visited Bing Nursery School, classes had not yet started for the fall, but we immediately and instinctively felt this would be the best spot for Cara. Its expansive classrooms were handsome and well-stocked with child-scale equipment. Each classroom opened onto its own half-acre patio and play area. On most days children could wander inside and out at will. Dr. D. Michelle Irwin, then director of Bing, was eager to have Cara enroll in the toddler class and seemed thoroughly committed to the idea of mainstreaming special children in "normal" classes. Cara's teacher-to-be, Lenore Thompson, was equally receptive. She and Cara seemed to hit it off immediately as they walked around the classroom and play area together. As Lenore took Cara's hand and walked over to the class pet, Duck-Duck, Paul and I sensed that we had found another Mattie, a natural teacher whose warmth brings out the best in children.

Our only reservation about Bing was that its toddler class met only two mornings a week. Would that provide enough stimulation for Cara, who had been receiving twice that much since she was one month old?

"I wish Mattie were here to help us decide what's best," I groaned to Paul one evening at supper.

"Well, why don't you call her," he said. I dialed. Busy. I waited several minutes and dialed again. Still busy. Her teenagers, Lynn and Laurie, must be monopolizing the phone, I thought. After several tries, I got through. Mattie was flabbergasted to hear from us.

Seven dollars and some change's worth of talk later, Mattie had put the whole thing in perspective and given us the support we needed to act on our intuitions. Bing sounded best to her, too, even if it met only two mornings each week. I told her that we were concerned that it wasn't enough and that we thought we should supplement Bing with something else.

"What area of Cara's development do you think we should concentrate on most?" I asked her.

"Speech. Her language is rolling along so beautifully right now that I'd hate to see it slow down," Mattie replied.

"But how do we find a good speech therapist?"

"Well, I can't tell you exactly," Mattie said, "But you'll know one when you find one."

A loquat tree grows in front of Gail Buschini's house in Menlo Park, California. To my New Englander's eyes, a loquat has leaves shaped like an elm but shinier. Its small smooth-skinned yellow fruit seems to contain more seeds than meat and it tastes quite tart. I had never heard of a loquat tree before living in California but, like many unexpected delights that we encountered there, the loquat and its owner came to have special meaning for Cara. Mattie had been right. We would recognize a good speech therapist when we found one. And fortunately we found one right away.

The morning after talking with Mattie, I called Romaine Sternad and told her that we appreciated her honest advice about enrolling Cara in a program where she would be challenged. I explained that we had decided on Bing Nursery School for that reason but that we were also looking for a speech therapist to give Cara some extra help. Could she recommend one? She gave me Gail Buschini's name and phone number.

Like Mattie and Lenore Thompson, Gail is a natural teacher. Gail related warmly to Cara, without any pretense or condescension. And like Mattie, she made Cara work. Finding Gail reminded me all over again of the streak of good luck threading through our lives. We had found Ken-Crest at the right moment. We were equally lucky to find Gail. Without Gail, Cara would have picked up bits and pieces of language at home and at school. But Gail opened up a world of language for Cara that, I am certain, she would never have acquired without Gail's help. Cara had begun to speak in short phrases and seemed to enjoy learning new words all the time. Gail walked onto Cara's stage when she was ripe for language stimulation in heavy doses. Jean Piaget called these receptive times "critical periods" and Dr. Maria Montessori called them "sensitive periods," terms I did not learn until later.

Language is a critical symbol system that allows us to process new information. A toddler is soaking up new information every waking hour. If a child cannot master language, he or she has a difficult time categorizing those experiences. At this point in Cara's development, language was one of her greatest strengths, as Gail observed midway through her year with Cara. We wanted to capitalize on this strength not only by giving her heaps of language to describe and make sense of her experiences, but also to give her a variety of experiences for which she would need to develop a greater vocabulary and language structure. So there were trips to the San Francisco Zoo, where she preferred chasing pigeons to looking at giraffes, trips across the Coast Ranges to picnic on the Pacific shore, and everyday walks to hang laundry on the community clothesline or to play in the sandpile. Our California year was an extraordinary opportunity for all of us to absorb new sights and experiences, but any toddler who is blossoming into the world of language can have experiences similar to Cara's. A trip to the grocery store can be a jackpot of language opportunity if the child is given the chance to point out, touch and name pineapples, celery, onions, boxes, bags, and cans. I silently weep when I see a harried parent whisking a young child through a market with no more conversation than "Don't touch that" or "I'm not buying that for you." And I rejoice when I see another parent say, "What's that? That's a red-skinned potato. It feels hard. Feel it. Please put four potatoes in the cart." It is so simple a language experience, yet so valuable.

Two afternoons a week, for forty-five minutes each session, Cara went to Gail's home with the enthusiasm most children have for going to the circus. (On days when she did not visit Gail, Cara often asked, "Gail and Toby house?" whenever we got into the car.) Toby Buschini, Gail's three-year-old son, would be waiting for Cara, riding his Big Wheel up and down the driveway or playing with Zinnia, the Buschinis' big black Labrador retriever. Gail often brought Toby into the sessions with Cara as a language model. His presence also helped Cara by supporting her use of language in interactions with other children.

For Cara going to Gail and Toby's was like going to a friend's house to play. But Gail used play and toys as jumping-off points for expanding Cara's language skills. A particular favorite was a set of Fisher-Price "little people." As Cara sat with Gail in front of a little A-frame dollhouse, they talked about Mr. Hooper or the mother or "the old man," as Cara insisted on calling a little figure in a cowboy hat, and about how the little people went "up" or "down" or would "sleep" or "eat," until Cara was expanding these individual words into phrases and then full sentences.

Many of Gail's teaching materials were Toby's toys but she also used a variety of commercially prepared materials used by speech and language teachers. These were used to teach concepts: shapes, colors, and numbers, as well as block patterns for sequencing and copying, sorting and matching, which were preparatory to concepts like "same" and "different." Gail worked on both Cara's receptive language and her expressive language—buzz words any parent whose child has had speech therapy knows. Receptive language refers to incoming language, or understanding what is heard. In that category, Gail worked with Cara on fol-

lowing one-, two- and three-part directions like, "Find Mr. Hooper and put him in bed." She would find objects or pictures of objects and move them according to Gail's verbal cues. Expressive language is outgoing language, simply the language one uses to express oneself. In that area, Gail worked with Cara to increase her vocabulary, to extend her sentence length, to build her language construction (such as linking adjective and noun, or linking noun, verb, and particle, as in "man go up"), to increase her use of forms and concepts (naming colors, shapes, numbers), and to spark her spontaneous speech in playing with toys, responding to questions, and interacting with other people.

At this stage in Cara's development, Gail emphasized the expansion of Cara's language more than the perfection of her articulation. Too much emphasis on clear pronounciation, Gail believed, could stifle Cara's spontaneous speech. Gail did not allow a poorly pronounced word to slip by, but neither did she drill Cara with articulation exercises. She gently helped Cara overcome an occasional reluctance to speak clearly or audibly when she was trying an expanded and often difficult word construction such as "man is big," "man sit on chair." In these instances, Cara would put her head down shyly and mumble softly or would not repeat a word or phrase Gail had offered as a model. Gail quietly but firmly repeated the word form and asked Cara to repeat it. If Cara did not, Gail dropped the matter, for the moment but brought it up again later. Like Mattie and other natural teachers I've observed, Gail never insulted Cara's emotional dignity. There was never any scolding or embarrassing. There was always warmth and support and praise.

The first thirty-five minutes of Gail and Cara's session were usually spent at a small table in Gail's teaching room. The last ten minutes Cara would climb into Gail's lap or sit beside her on a sofa while Gail read. This story time was a less formal opportunity than the previous thirty-five minutes for Gail to model sentences for Cara, to expand her own sentences, and to add vocabulary. One afternoon when I arrived early to pick up Cara, I sat in on the last portion of a session. It opened my eyes. Gail did not simply read a story verbatim, cover to cover. She got Cara involved in the story. Gail read each page and then asked Cara questions about the pictures—"Where are the butterflies? How many butterflies are there? What color are the boy's shoes? What is that rabbit doing?" I felt

like banging my head on the nearest wall. I had been reading books to
Cara for nearly three years and had just been reading the words. Occasionally I asked Cara something about the pictures, but I had rarely
stopped to do what Gail was doing systematically. The words on the page
were secondary in Gail's approach. Cara's involvement was primary. It
was all so obvious but I had missed it. I went home newly resolved to
read to Cara in Gail's fashion—and to read this way to David as well.

Our year in California was one of the state's worst drought years. Stanford turned off its underground sprinkler system that formerly kept the
grass beyond our patio a lush green. Everyone tried to conserve water. I
used dishwater to keep houseplants from parching. While the drought
situation was serious for many permanent Californians, we secretly, almost guiltily, enjoyed every opportunity to be outdoors. I had been told
in the autumn that boots were an absolute necessity for Bing Nursery
children in January when the play area customarily became awash in
mud. But by January the drought had eliminated any need for boots.

Nearly every afternoon after a nap or session with Gail, Cara, David and
I spent several hours outside. Somehow Cara managed to log plenty of
"Sesame Street" hours, though, either in the late afternoons or on mornings when she did not attend Bing. I have never harbored more than an
ounce of guilt for using the electronic babysitter as long as the show was
"Sesame Street," "Mr. Rogers" or "The Electric Company." Cara benefited
tremendously from them. She watched "Sesame Street" with complete
concentration for its entire hour, unlike David and many other children
who watch it in stretches, wander off and return for another dose. Cara's
rapt attention made me wonder initially if this was a totally passive experience for her. Was she a sponge soaking up all these electronic waves
and sounds? But I soon realized that she could give back what she saw
and heard in expressive language.

In March of that California year, a month after Cara turned three, she
was playing with some letter blocks. She pointed to the F and said
"friend." She picked up a K block and said "kangaroo." Amazed, I pointed
to a C and asked, "What is C for?" "Chicken," she said. And so it went, G
for goat, W for wagon. It was my first recognition that she was beginning

to understand that letters were more than shapes to be recognized and named. They were symbols for something else. She was not repeating what she was seeing on a page or picture but was calling forth an object from her memory to link with the appropriate letter! I suppose this marked the beginning of her reading career. Thank you, "Sesame Street."

Paul's fellowship allowed fellows and their spouses to audit Stanford courses. Living right on campus gave Paul and me few logistical problems for juggling child care and courses. At the beginning of each quarter Paul selected his courses first—it was his fellowship after all—and then I selected courses at other times. Paul often sped home on his bike over the flat terrain just in time for me to ride off to my course. One of the few rainy days that year, Paul put on a red-hooded parka, and, as he mounted the bike on the patio, Cara looked out the window and dubbed him "Spiderman Daddy," a nickname that stuck a long while.

I sampled a variety of courses on subjects that I would never have made the time to study on my own: African art, twentieth-century American art, poetry. I also wanted to learn more about subjects close at hand so I audited two psychology courses, "Early Experience" and "Exceptional Children." I felt I had one foot in each course. I pedaled off at 8:00 A.M. three mornings a week during the winter quarter to hear a leading experimental psychologist, Dr. Seymour Levine, talk about "critical periods," "infantile stimulation," isolation, stimulus deprivation, and trauma— all terms that applied to rats, mice and monkeys used in laboratory experiments designed to suggest the influence of early experience on their later development. It was a bit of a cart-before-the-horse experience because many of the experiments and their conclusions reminded me of what I had already observed in Cara's early intervention program at Ken-Crest. When Dr. Levine talked about stimulating rats from one to twenty-two days of age with brief electric shocks, I drew eerie analogies to stimulating infants like Cara with early exercises. When he talked about how the stimulated rats showed greater exploration of their environment than the control group of baby rats left alone, unhandled, I could appreciate the parallel with babies stimulated very young.

Dr. Levine spent several sessions on the subject of "maternal deprivation syndrome": abnormal postures and movements, face rubbing, thumbsucking, rocking, motivational disturbances (excessive fearfulness of any change in the environment, for example), poor integration of motor patterns, and deficiencies in social communication. Although Dr. Levine was lecturing about monkeys, I could not help but abstract these experiments to the human level. Many of the developmentally delayed children I had observed at Ken-Crest and other programs had been deprived of human contact and stimulation in their earliest days, either from neglect or because the infant had a medical problem that required isolation. I thought of all the children who have been institutionalized at a very young age. No wonder society has such low expectations of the mentally retarded. So many were probably showing "maternal deprivation syndrome" in addition to their genetic shortcomings. And, to top that, much of what has been written by professionals in the field of mental retardation has been based on institutionalized people. Once again my belief in rearing a delayed child at home whenever possible was reinforced.

In the spring quarter at Stanford, I audited Dr. Gloria Leiderman's course, "Exceptional Children." I was at least a decade older than the other students in this undergraduate course and the only one who had an exceptional child. I was amazed at how little exposure these undergraduates had had to handicapped children, and at their misconceptions about them.

Dr. Leiderman required her students to become involved personally by observing one exceptional child at least three different times and integrating these observations with their readings into a research paper. I offered to let a student observe Cara as a subject. The student was a quiet freshman who sat in on a session between Gail and Cara, a morning at Bing, and an afternoon at home. As she was taking notes on Cara's playing at home, Cara accidentally knocked a small doll off the coffee table and said, in a tone of voice befitting the occasion, "Oh, shit." The freshman looked up from her notebook, glanced cautiously at me. I said, "Yes, you heard her correctly, I'm afraid." This was the first time I had heard Cara use that word. Children have a knack for always picking the best moment though. The freshman went back to her notetaking and I wondered if she included Cara's appropriate remark in her research paper.

While Paul and I took courses, Cara flourished at Bing. Unlike many of her "normal" classmates, who had never been in a school setting before, she did not have the separation problems that most toddlers have when leaving home for the first time. No clinging to my leg on her part. She went right to work upon entering the classroom. She went off independently through a series of "jobs" until we picked her up at noon. As Paul and I watched her, we enjoyed a rich sense of her budding independence. She was very comfortable and confident at Bing. At Ken-Crest we had been spoiled by almost daily comments about what Cara was doing, where she needed help and reinforcement, what her next goal would be. There was nothing comparable at Bing. But why should I have expected there to be? Ken-Crest offered a small group setting where each child had one or more developmental problems and each was treated very individually. At Bing some twenty two- and three-year-olds were playing, exploring materials, learning to socialize with—that is, not grab from—each other. They were normal, all-American toddlers. At noon parents walked into the classroom, retrieved their children and left. There was little parent-teacher conversation. I missed that at first but gradually resolved myself to the difference. This was not, after all, a Ken-Crest. Cara was in the real world of nursery school.

Gail visited Bing one December morning to observe Cara in a classroom setting. She concluded that Cara was an observer more than a participant. As Gail watched Cara outdoors with the other children, she noted that Cara did not do all the climbing of slides and jungle-gyms that the others did, but seemed to watch the other children. Gail felt that Cara knew her physical limitations. When she felt ready and confident after watching these normal role-models, she would try to do what they did.

Gail also noticed that Cara did not initiate conversations with other children. She answered if another child spoke to her but she was far from being a chatterbox. This is not unusual for children at this age but in Cara's case, Gail felt, we should encourage her to talk more with her classmates. Gail suggested that we invite a classmate to play at home with Cara so that a one-to-one situation might develop into a chattier relationship back in school. We did this a few times, but before we saw any marked effect, it was time to pack up for our return East. The situation continues to this day, when Cara is eight. She still works independently

in class, talking to other children when they speak to her but very seldom starting a conversation. Her teachers have tried to set up situations where she would be more likely to converse, but she still seems to prefer to work on her own. I suspect this goes back to Cara's roots at Ken-Crest. From the beginning she was encouraged to perform tasks independently and she continues to take the classroom seriously. When asked what she did in school today, she always replies in terms of "work": "I did good work today. I worked hard at my writing." But I wonder, too, if her reticence to chitchat with classmates is not partly another case of her sensing her limitations. Other eight-year-olds talk a mile a minute. She talks more slowly. Others are using more sophisticated concepts than she. She must be aware of this difference.

Midway through her year at Bing, Cara's class lost Lenore Thompson. She had the opportunity to return to a graduate school program that she felt she needed professionally. We were sorry to see Lenore go because we had felt very secure with her as Cara's head teacher. It was the first time we had lost someone in whom we had made a sizable emotional investment. Mattie had been such a constant in Cara's life for two and a half years that, when we found Lenore, we had expected without thinking that she would succeed Mattie in Cara's life for the nine months at Stanford. Our disappointment in losing Lenore showed us how much more hope and trust parents of a retarded child place in the child's teacher than parents of non-retarded children. In later years David would also lose a teacher to whom we and he had become attached but it would not be the same loss, because we knew that David would make it one way or another. We were more protective of Cara than David: David is a survivor, Cara needs help to survive; David's having good teachers was less important to us than Cara's having them. Unfair, yes, but true.

Lenore Thompson was followed by Jim Cushing, a bright, sensitive young man who brought the year to a smooth conclusion. At spring's end when we were beginning to pack for our return home, Jim wrote the following report for Cara's future teachers:

Attitudinal directiveness: *The concept that most distinguishes Cara's choice and direction of exploration is self-determination. She generally enters the room ahead of her father or mother at a fast gait. She moves directly to her cubby and begins to take off her outer coat or sweater. She takes out her name tag and hands it to her parents to put on for her. When she has finished she motions to her parents a good-bye and moves to the activity of her choice with the speed and direction of a firm conviction of her needs. She is independent and assertive in her actions and exploration, as though she came with her own agenda for her day's work. She plays and works methodically, moving from one activity to another as the moment moves her, at times spending 30 to 45 minutes in intense play, concentrating on her work like a dancer practicing for her premiere. She takes special joy not only in her activity but also in her developing skills of fine and gross motor movement. Often her involvement in dramatic play is simultaneously joined with a constant running narrative of her actions and thoughts, as though she were finding joy in her ability to verbalize her own actions and incorporate these into her continued play.*

Activity likes: *Cara is especially fond of role playing and testing her developing skills of coordination, balance, and problem solving. She is assertive in her actions and often demonstrates a greater control over her environment than the other children. She loves books and after a long day of active exploration will locate herself in the language arts area with a book. There she will sit alone, with others, or by a teacher, opening a book and giving a monologue on the contents. She spends time working with materials that are highly malleable such as Play Doh, art projects and painting. She doesn't spend much time with small manipulatives that are closed as to function.*

Adult/child interaction: *She does not seek out other children but will respond to parallel play and initiative on the part of other children. I have noticed over the last couple of months that her language is developing nicely and this has allowed her to interact more clearly with the other children. She is a leader unto herself and is liked and plays well with the other girls in the class. She is highly sensitive to the distress of other children and I have seen her assist a child in need. Her interactions with adults is dependent on their location and her involvement in the activity at hand. Her initiation of verbal communication centers around her involvement in an activity in short one- or two-word sentences. She grasps not only the activity but also the social involvement of others. Cara is a conserver in the sense that each action appears to have been thought out before hand. She moves steadfastly in the direction of her needs and desires. I have not seen her cry when involved in a conflict with others, and her language development is assisting her in making her rights known to others. She is moving from a passive social agent to an active capable individual.*

Autonomous power: *She has great control in her movement and only appears mad, angry, sad, when she makes a mistake in judgment and may fall. These times are followed by a moment of anguish, as if to say "how stupid of me to make this mistake." To my way of thinking, she is developing positively along all lines. She is a joy to know and watch and has demonstrated behaviors that are a great model for the other children.*

Our California year was not without at least one battle on the bureaucratic front. Early in the year we had registered with the area "regional center" for mental health and retardation. We sought payment for Cara's nursery school and speech therapy, to which a retarded child was entitled in California at that time. Throughout that year we received forms in blue and pink and yellow and letters peppered with words like "vendorized" and "provider of care." After many go-rounds, the regional social work counselor wrote to Bing Nursery School and acknowledged that "we mistakenly told them [Cara's parents] that Bing was not vendorized by the State. I have since learned that Bing is vendorized to receive Regional Center funding. Therefore, you will soon be receiving our billing forms to cover Cara's attendance from 1-24-77 to 6-15-77 at the rate of $120 a quarter which is the rate we have established by the State Department of Health."

"Vendorized" made me imagine a nursery school in the shape of a vending machine—put in a quarter, push a button, and out pops a toddler covered with finger paint. Put in another quarter, push another button, and out pops another kid sticky with clay.

Though the vendorizing matter was a classic bureaucratic mix-up, the real reason the state finally came through with Cara's tuition reimbursement and part of her speech therapy fees, as a state social worker later conceded privately, was the fact that the end of the fiscal year was approaching and the State Department of Health had money lying in its coffers. In mid-July, when we were back in Philadelphia, our $225 refund for Cara's Bing tuition arrived in the mail.

As we prepared to leave Stanford that May, Paul and I reflected on our nine months there. Stanford had offered a palm and eucalyptus grove to relax and rethink what we were doing and where our lives were going. But it recharged our batteries to be returning to the real world. I became acutely aware near the end of our Stanford vacation, that we had witnessed very little poverty, no bag ladies hovering near underground vents to keep warm as on a cold Philadelphia night, no "urban decay" of boarded-up warehouses and rowhouses, even very few old people. As I stopped for a traffic light on a Palo Alto corner one afternoon that spring, I noticed a frail old lady in gloves and flowered hat. Such a sight would be commonplace back home but it was so rare for me at that moment that I was actually startled. Leaving the homogeneous campus world, pleasant though it was, was not that difficult. I looked forward to returning to Philadelphia.

The most enduring California experience for Cara was Gail's teaching. When she began seeing Gail, Cara had a vocabulary of seventy-five to a hundred words, which she usually used alone or in two-word combinations. Occasionally there was a short sentence like "Daddy cook outside," a wonderfully Californian statement. Eight months later Cara's vocabulary was so vast that we had given up counting. Gail estimated that it had grown to two hundred fifty to three hundred words used in three- and four-word combinations. Most important, Cara's use of language had expanded enormously. She was using pronouns correctly as well as a good number of prepositions. Her articulation was much sharper and, most delightfully, her language had taken on a spontaneous quality that continually surprised us.

Paul and I met with Gail for a final report on Cara's progress. Gail told us to watch Cara's control of the tip of her tongue, that she was not using the tip well and should be encouraged to improve. She cautioned us to listen carefully to Cara's language. "Notice what word forms she does not use and help her with those she's starting to use," Gail suggested. "She'll need more speech work, probably for a year or so more." We asked Gail what to look for in selecting a speech therapist for the future. Gail's very practical advice was to "observe people as they're working with kids and look for whether it works for Cara."

Cara slid down Toby's sliding board for the last time and ate her last loquat from Gail's tree. Gail made a book for Cara to take home on the plane. She had drawn pictures and written sentences about the things she, Cara and Toby had shared, including the line, "Cara ate lots of loquats." Cara brought back a rich linguistic treasure from California. I brought back a few loquat seeds from Gail's tree. As I type these words, I can look over at the window sill and see our four-inch loquat growing in a pot.

SEVEN

"I Do It Myself"

On returning to Philadelphia, one of our priorities was seeing Mattie again. When she came for dinner one summer evening, Cara was shy at first. She slowly warmed up and climbed into Mattie's lap as Mattie and I talked. Cara snuggled in, and it was as if she had never left.

After dinner Mattie came upstairs with us and I drew a bath for Cara and David. Until this time Cara had steadfastly refused to abandon her little potty chair for the regular toilet. She seemed timid about sitting up so high, with her feet dangling off the floor, on a hole much too big for her. I had been encouraging her to try the toilet but I had not pushed the issue. As Cara undressed that evening, I asked her if she wanted to go to the potty.

"I sit on the big potty," she answered. I was shocked but I did not let her know it. I lifted her up onto the "big potty" and continued to talk to Mattie in an even tone. But I interjected, as if it were a normal part of the continuing conversation, "Mattie, you are witnessing a first." When Cara finished, we both gave her a hearty round of applause and praised her as "a big lady who can sit on the big potty."

Why did Cara choose that particular time to take this giant step? I can draw only one conclusion: she did it for Mattie. She remembered that this was the woman she enjoyed pleasing, the one for whom she would risk something untried and possibly difficult. The next morning I put the upstairs and downstairs potties away until David would need them a year later. Cara asked for them several times in the next few days, but I told her that I had put them away because she was a big lady now.

Finding a new school for Cara was also high on our agenda after returning to Philadelphia. Cara had flourished at Bing, and we wanted to find her another good mainstreaming situation among normal children. Most nursery schools are happy places, decked out in rainbow colors with smiling suns and flowers painted on the walls. The children play and paint and learn songs and ABCs in a fairly relaxed, unstructured fashion. I wondered if Cara would do better in a Montessori class where attractive learning materials beg a young child to get involved, to touch, see, smell, to create her own learning adventures from concrete sensory experiences. Another appeal of a Montessori education for us was the fact that Maria Montessori first used her approach to early education with "defective" children, as slow children were called at the beginning of this century.

From my first visit to a Montessori school before we went to California, I also thought that the mixed ages of a Montessori class would be beneficial for Cara. She could progress at her own rate among children about her age without feeling an emphasis on doing a particular skill at a particular age. I was especially interested in finding a Montessori school that had elementary grades as well as primary (most Montessori schools in this country are primary only), because I hoped that Cara could have the consistency of nine or ten years under the same roof. Perhaps that was not the most realistic or logical of hopes, but when parents of a handicapped child find a good program and fine teachers they want to perpetuate that success as long as possible.

We visited three Montessori schools that went through sixth grade. Two seemed good. The third was outstanding. The Children's House, The Gladwyne Montessori School, is seven miles from our home but well worth the carpooling. My first impression of it was that it looked the way a school should look—an old fieldstone building that once was a public school. The room where Cara was to spend her primary years was a one-room schoolhouse back in 1884. Fireplaces in that and two adjacent rooms were the sole source of heat years ago. More recently they have served as nooks for the class guinea pig and rabbit cages. All of the older classrooms have polished wood floors and high windows. Perhaps because it reminded me of the old grammar school I attended and my father before me, The Children's House made me feel at home.

But far more important than its physical appearance, the school projected a warmth and good feeling about children. Its headmistress, Kathleen Dzura, was enthusiastic about accepting Cara because she felt that mainstreaming a child with Down's syndrome would not only help the child but would also benefit the other children by exposing them to someone who was different. She told me of another child with Down's syndrome who had attended a Montessori school until she was thirteen. When she left, most of her academic skills were at an eight-year-old's level. There was no stigma about the child's working below her age level, Kathy said. She worked at her own pace, and she fit in socially with the younger children in the elementary grades, until she became at age twelve, decidedly bigger than her eight- and nine-year-old peers.

Kathy asked me to bring Cara in to meet her teacher-to-be, Ann Schwarz. We visited on a hot, humid morning and I felt wilted, but Ann met us at school in a crisp blue-and-white dress. She looked tan and healthy and cool. I immediately liked her direct approach with me and her gentle manner with Cara. As soon as we entered Kathy Dzura's office, Cara pulled a puzzle off a low shelf, turned out the pieces and began putting them back together. She finished the puzzle, put it back on the shelf (Had she read that this is what Montessori children are supposed to do?), and selected a book. When she sat on the sofa to look at the book, Ann sat beside her and softly asked her questions about the pictures. Cara answered quietly and they seemed to hit it off instantly. Near the end of the interview, Ann asked me if Cara was always so independent. Ann knew other children with Down's syndrome but never before had she met a three-year-old Little Miss Business.

Cara's first year in a Montessori class was a joy. Although she was one of the youngest in a class of twenty-seven children ranging from three to six years, Cara swung right into class activity. "Cara's power of concentration is overwhelming," Ann said. "She spends over an hour on a given activity."

While she was happy to be absorbed in work of her own, Cara was at first shy with the other children, just as she had been at Bing. Eventually she became more outgoing and acquired two particular friends, Susannah and Pamela—or "Camela" as Cara insisted on pronouncing the name. Ann found it interesting that five-year-old Pamela chose to become Cara's big friend because Pamela herself had been very retiring and shy during her first year in the class.

Cara's classmates did not notice that Cara was different until she had to participate in walking on the line, a Montessori group activity in which children carefully place one foot in front of the other on an inch-wide line taped to the floor. Here Cara's lack of coordination stood out. Ann handled the situation adroitly: Cara was special in this area just as Susannah was special because she wore glasses and Cherie was special because her skin color happened to be black. Ann's attitude, which the children absorbed, was simply that all children are different. In Cara's case, the rest of the children not only accepted her difference, but competed to help her when help was needed.

A Montessori classroom is arranged by subject: language arts, math and practical life. The fourth main area of the Montessori primary curriculum, grace and courtesy, has no specific locale but is practiced throughout the room. It still amazes me, even after five years of observing Montessori classes, how Montessori children will carefully walk around another child's work that is spread out on a floor mat, excuse themselves if they accidentally bump into another child, and willingly serve snacks to visitors and each other. (Cara's favorite was food serving, Ann reported, and she wouldn't take no for an answer when it came time to share a snack with everyone.)

One morning midway through Cara's first year at The Children's House, Mattie came with me to visit. She wanted to see Cara in action. After we had observed through the one-way window quite a while, Mattie remarked, "I can't believe it. Those children are so nice to each other. Look how much touching is going on." She was right. A child would briefly lay a hand on another's shoulder as he maneuvered around that child. A pair of children would hold hands as they walked down the hallway. And teachers would put an arm around a child when teaching a new activity. "I am impressed," Mattie concluded. "You don't see that in very many preschool classes."

Cara spent much of her first year in the practical life area, which is usual for first-year Montessori children. She loved to wash things in the sink, polish shoes and silverware, pour beans or rice from tiny pitchers into bowls, wash tabletops, and attempt zipper, snap and button frames even though these frames were difficult for her. Because Ann had some experience with Down's children, she knew how important large and small muscle control is for their development, and guided Cara in these practical life and sensorial exercises as well as in her working with clay and other art materials.

The practical life experiences give a young child an opportunity to master the surrounding environment by caring for it. The child learns there is an order to doing things. You do not simply slop water on the tabletop; you get your materials together and proceed to wet the sponge, wet the tabletop, apply soap, rub the tabletop in a circular motion, rinse, dry, and put away the cleaning materials. The child gains a sense of accomplishment and confidence from exercises like these. They offer opportunities to develop fine and gross motor skills as well.

Dr. Montessori believed that no one teaches a child—the child learns by doing. Yet a young child needs "help to help himself." In introducing a new task or skill, a Montessori teacher uses an approach which Dr. Montessori adopted from Edouard Seguin, a pioneer in educating the retarded. It is called a three-period lesson and it works particularly well when done slowly and repeatedly with a developmentally delayed child. For instance, the first period establishes an identity, or associates the sense perception with its name. The teacher presents two rods and says, "This is short. This is long." The second period tests the child's recognition of the object corresponding to the name: "Which is long?" "Which is short?" If the child answers correctly, the rods are mixed and the questions repeated to strengthen the association. The third period verifies that the child can recall the name corresponding to the object. When shown the short rod, the child is asked, "What is this?"

The three-part approach is standard operating procedure whenever a Montessori teacher introduces a new learning activity. It works well with bright children and, when repeated more often, with slower children.

Before we left California, Gail Buschini had asked me to send her an occasional language sample so that she could keep up with Cara's progress. In November, six months after Gail had last seen Cara, I sat down with pencil and notepad to record a sample of Cara's around-the-house chatter. I had previously tried to do so with a tape recorder but I could not do it surreptitiously enough. Cara was too distracted by the buttons and the microphone.

When she noticed me taking notes, Cara asked, "Mommy, you the teacher?"

"Yes, I'm the teacher," I lied.

"Mommy, stop that. Now stop that. You hurt me." (I was smoothing her hair from under her collar.) "What's his name here?" she asked, pointing to a picture in a nearby newspaper. "What's her name?"

"Sally," I said, pulling a name from the air just to keep the conversation going. The rest went like this:

Oh, my goodness. . . . Jack be nimble. Jack be quick. Jack jump over the candlestick. . . . [Picking up the mail] I got a letter. The mailman came. This is for you, Mommy. This be for Daddy. It's Daddy's letter. . . . What's that? ("My tea," I answered.) Mommy, read me a story. ("Okay, get me a book.") Okay, please. ("Where shall we read?") Right here. Mommy, I can read to you. This is your book. This is for you. [We read.] Mommy, I want some juice. [I get the juice.] Jack and Jill went up the hill [she completes the verse]. [I give her the juice.] Thank you. That's juice, yeah. Cow, want some? [She puts the cup to the mouth of a toy cow.] He likes juice. You want some, girl [to a doll]? Hi, little boy. Watch this [she sets the boy doll on the cow]. . . . Where David go? Where's David? ("David is sleeping.") Oh. . . . A, B, C, D [she sings the entire alphabet song to the cow]. . . . Stand up, cow. Mommy, I outside. ("No, Cara, it's raining outside. Everything is wet.") I go that way [pointing to the door]. I go that way. ("The door is locked, Cara.") No, in that door. ("Everything is wet out there.") No! [She's getting ornery.] I can't. When's it time to go? ("We're not going anywhere now, honey.")

[A few moments later she resumes her chatter.] I going to be the teacher. I be the teacher [reaching for my pad and pencil]. Mommy, I can spell. I want to spell myself. I want to writing myself. [I give her paper and pencil.] Thank you. I draw [she scribbles a while]. . . . Mommy, let's go a picklick [translation: picnic]. We have food in the basket. Mommy, I want some food in the basket. ("What food would you like?") Raisins and grapes. Mackin [translation: napkin] for yourself. We have a mat [a blanket or tablecloth for the picnic]? Yes, Mommy, come over here. Where's the mat go? [We spread the mat on the living room floor.] ("What's that, Cara?") A lunch. Yes, let's see. Oh,

this is the raisins, and the mackin. Where's yours? There, we have a picklick together. I open a lunch [sandwich] . . . now, a raisins. There . . . there, open your mat [spreading my napkin out for me]. You eat all by yourself. This is for you. You like it? Mommy, you want a apple?

[After the picnic had been cleaned up, I went back to collecting more of the language sample.] I'm three. I'm three years old. And I'm big. Where's David? What's David doing? He's drawing, I think. You are my sister, David. ("No, he's your brother, Cara.") Oh, yeah. I love you. I love you, baby David. He love me. He's cute little boy. Mommy, what time is it? ("It's 2:20.") Oh, David crying. ("Why is he crying, Cara?") He bump his head. Poor David. I want to kiss you. I kiss him on the head.

The language sample abruptly ended with David's need for comfort. When I typed it up for Gail, I was surprised to find how much Cara's language had grown. Listening to her everyday, I had taken much of it for granted. Transcribing the sample showed me that she was using a lot more word forms and experimenting with variations like "Where David go? Where's David?" as if trying them on for size to see how they fit.

The same day I took the language sample, Cara began playing with my typewriter. "Me type, Mommy?" She began banging the keys with her palms. I wiggled my index finger and suggested that she push the Y key with her finger. She did. We went through the keyboard, one letter and one finger at a time. That incident was a chance to turn simple play into a spontaneous learning exercise. In this case, pushing typewriter keys with her index finger could strengthen her fine motor control.

When Cara was younger, we once found her pulling Paul's socks onto her tiny feet. It was a cute scene but it was also another chance happening that can turn into a learning experience. She seemed to be telling us by her actions, "Look, I have trouble putting on my socks. Why can't I practice with these big ones? They're easier for me." Certainly Paul's socks were easier for her to manipulate than her own, but the process of opening the sock top, putting in the foot with the heel to the back, and pulling up the sock required the same coordination that she would have to use in putting on her own little socks. She was deeply into a I-do-it-all-by-myself stage at the time and took great pride in such accomplishments.

Incidents like these pop up all the time. I am sure that I have missed millions of them because my mind has been on other things. When I have noticed and made use of these opportunities, I have been warmed by a sense of satisfaction that both Cara and I share.

Cara's Montessori class met five mornings a week. While that was considerably more frequent than at Bing, we felt that she should continue some speech and language therapy on a one-to-one basis. The Philadelphia School District's program called PEACH (Prescriptive Educational Approach for Children with Handicaps) offered a speech and hearing service for preschoolers. One cold October day, Cara and I arrived at the PEACH center on the second floor of an old public school building. Cara slowly made her way up the long flight of steep stairs—stairs designed for older children and adults were a challenge for her three-year-old legs. I filled out a lengthy background information form while Cara was tested by a young speech therapist named Mrs. Harris. "You can call me 'Harris.' Most of the children do," she told Cara.

Cara had not been through such a comprehensive battery of tests before. She responded to Mrs. Harris's questions comfortably. For her, it was just another one-on-one session like the many she had spent with Gail. After a full morning of tests, Mrs. Harris compiled the results and wrote up a report in which she gave this summary:

Based on the data collected from this evaluation, Cara's speech and language development are age appropriate at the present time. In accordance with the test interpretation of the Arizona Articulation Proficiency Scale a normal articulation pattern has emerged for Cara's age. Informal observation of Cara revealed good communication intent and interaction with her environment. She was able to orient herself from one task to another with structure and showed a good attention span until completion of each task presented to her. Based on results of the Denver Developmental Screening Test, Cara functioned at age level in personal-social growth. Fine motor adaptive skills were age appropriate within this test structure with the exception that she was unable to pick the longest line from a set of two lines. Language skills were age appropriate with the exception that Cara could not recognize colors.

*Cara could comprehend concepts of cold, tired and hungry, give identi-
fying information about herself as well as comprehend prepositions
giving a specific direction.*

*Based on the results of the Carrow Auditory Comprehension of Lan-
guage Test, Cara scored an age equivalency of 3.5 years. [She was 3.7 at
the time of the test.] Areas of weakness closest to her developmental
level of learning were in personal pronouns (number) and recognition
of pictures using adjectives. Receptive Vocabulary continued to be age
appropriate based on the results of the Peabody Picture Vocabulary Test
where Cara scored a mental age of 3.8 years.*

Cara could not qualify for the PEACH program, Mrs. Harris explained, because "we are not mandated to accept children who are so close to
normal."

Catch-22! Cara had scored well on these tests because she had extra
stimulation and language help for more than three years. Yet she could
not qualify for more help, because the earlier help had been so successful. I might have argued with the school district bureaucrats that Cara
could backslide without continued help. As a taxpayer, I could understand their giving priority to children whose speech and language needs
were greater than Cara's, but there was no waiting list. Paul and I saw no
point in engaging the school district in battle, especially since it would
be a war of words like "mandated."

As long as we could squeeze enough from the family budget, Paul and I
decided we would find a private speech and language pathologist. The
first one we tried came to the house a few times and did activities with
Cara that were far below her level. I did not have to be a speech pathologist myself to recognize that this young woman was inexperienced. We
then found Beverly Kaplan-Kraut, a very professional woman whose approach with Cara was pleasant yet businesslike. While Gail had emphasized language, Beverly stressed tongue and jaw control to improve
Cara's articulation, especially of *t* and *d* sounds. She suggested to Cara
that she call her tongue "Tommy Turtle" and that Tommy's house was
Cara's mouth. Her teeth were the doors of the house. "Keep Tommy Turtle inside his house," Beverly reminded Cara when she was eating and
swallowing. Beverly also had a clever way of monitoring how Cara used

her tongue while she drank liquids. She sliced the top half of a plastic cup at a diagonal angle. As Cara drank from the uncut rim, Beverly looked over her shoulder into the cup to see if Cara's tongue protruded as she began to drink. We have long since stopped using Beverly's shocking pink cup that way, but it still sits on the cupboard shelf with other drinking glasses. "What's *that?*" exclaims many a surprised visitor to our kitchen.

To firm up the muscle tone of Cara's tongue, Beverly brushed the tip of Cara's tongue with a toothbrush for about five seconds, rested, and repeated the brushing exercise twice more. This heightened Cara's awareness of her tongue tip and helped her make clearer "T" and "D" sounds. Beverly also suggested using an ice cube to rub on the tip of the tongue for the same purpose.

Cara had a tendency to thrust her jaw forward as she brought a cup or spoon to her mouth. To correct this, Beverly used what she called "jaw control." It simply meant that Beverly or Paul or I gently but firmly held Cara's jaw in place with our index finger across the front of her chin and our thumb on her jawbone near her ear. This exercise, which is commonly used with young children who have cerebral palsy, helps to stabilize the jaw in a straight position. At first Cara wiggled and balked at this exercise, but we talked to her as we held her jaw in place and reassured her that we were just helping to keep her jaw quiet. As we held this jaw position, she took a drink or spoonful of food. After each swallow or chew, we encouraged her to close her mouth by gently moving the chin and lower lip upward. As we had with all Cara's other exercises since infancy, we gradually removed this control as she began to control her jaw and tongue on her own. As we withdrew this support, we reminded her with a verbal cue: "Keep Tommy Turtle in his house."

Beverly also assigned homework. Cara and I were to find pictures of *t* words, tape them in her notebook, and practice saying words that begin with *t*. The *d* sound ("the woodpecker sound," as Beverly called it) followed *t* and we repeated the homework with *d* words. Beverly found a number of short poems with *t* and *d* words for Cara to recite: "Tit-tat-toe, round and round we'll go. Tit-tat-toe, round the maple tree."

Visual memory was another area where Cara showed some weakness. To strengthen this, Beverly set up exercises that Cara thought were fun. Beverly would line up three or four toys, ask Cara to look closely at the toys and then, as Cara watched, remove one toy and rearrange the order of the others. "What's missing?" Beverly asked Cara. The next step was to present three or four toys, ask Cara to cover her eyes, remove one toy, and ask what was missing. Another variation was to set out three toys (or any household objects), ask Cara to observe them, close her eyes, add a new toy or object, and then ask her what had changed in the collection.

Everyday situations present similar opportunities to enhance visual memory. For instance, when I took Cara grocery shopping, I asked her to name items we were selecting as she placed them in the cart. When we arrived home, I would ask her what we bought at the grocery store.

When she was four and five, Cara had considerable difficulty with visual memory exercises. If I would place three pictures in a row, show them to her, then turn them over slowly and in order, she could not pick out the one I asked for. I found that if she named the pictures in order when they were face up, she had an easier time finding the requested one after I turned them all over. This led me to believe that adding the oral input to the auditory—both saying and hearing the picture's name—helped her visual memory. Even so, she had difficulty if there were more than three pictures involved.

We never drilled her with these visual memory exercises. Paul and I did them with her sporadically as we remembered to do them. But somehow they must have worked, for her visual memory gradually improved. A month before she turned six, I rearranged six pictures on our living room and hall walls one evening after Cara and David had gone to sleep. When Cara came downstairs the next morning, the rooms were still dim but she immediately noticed that a different picture was on the front hall wall. She asked me, "Who did that?" I confessed. She led me to the spot where that picture had been, noted the picture now in its place, went to the spot where that one had been, and so on until she had retraced all the steps of my somewhat complex six-way rearrangement. I was impressed with her memory skill but I also realized that her memory is much sharper for a concrete experience than for something as abstract and out-of-context as our game of picture-scrambling.

Beverly worked with Cara nearly every Saturday morning for an hour in our playroom, in front of the mirror or on the floor, through the spring after Cara's fourth birthday. Then she had the opportunity to leave the area for a speech pathologist's internship that she very much wanted. She had been most successful with Cara and we were sorry to lose her. Once again, we consulted Mattie about whether we should find another speech therapist for Cara. Mattie felt that Cara was doing so well that "maybe she needs a rest period. I wouldn't like to see her pushed to the point where she couldn't succeed. Keep her developing normally. But if we put too much pressure on her, maybe speech would become negative to her." Mattie's philosophy all along had been to help a delayed child function (a word Mattie uses a lot) as close to normal as possible. "I'm not too comfortable pushing them beyond that point," she has often said.

After Beverly left, we did not look for another speech and language pathologist right away. But one found us. The county "intermediate unit," an agency which provides special education services to private- as well as public school handicapped children since the 1975 enactment of the Education for All Handicapped Children Act (Public Law 94-142), had assigned a speech therapist to The Children's House that spring. Under local regulations, a child could qualify for such service once they turned five years of age. That rule, I felt, belonged alongside the word "mandated" in the bureaucrats' wastebasket. Could not many problems be alleviated before age five? I thought Cara was living proof of that. The Education for All Handicapped Children Act had a convenient loophole for states that did not wish to extend its benefits to very young children. Enacted in 1975, the law set a deadline of September 1978, by which time a free, appropriate education had to be provided for all handicapped children between the ages of three and eighteen. The law also provided that the coverage be extended to age twenty-one by September 1980. But there was an exception: ages three to five and eighteen to twenty-one could be omitted in states where provision of public education for children in these age groups does not agree with state law or practice. Pennsylvania was one of those states.

The county intermediate unit assigned Patricia Bainbridge to The Children's House and three other non-public schools. Although Cara had nearly a year to go before she turned five and could qualify for Patricia's speech therapy, we were so impressed with Patricia that we asked her if she could see Cara as a private client. For a few times in the late spring and through the following fall, Patricia worked with Cara in two short sessions a week. Patricia became another Mattie for us, another person whose professional judgment we trust and respect. Witty, often flip with me, she is direct with Cara:

"Draw a square just like this one right here, Cara."

"I'll try."

"Not 'try,' Cara. *Do* it. You can do it."

Like Mattie, Patricia has a philosophy about working with delayed children that I fully support. "I say, get as much out of them as you can without frustrating them. If I have to use rewards, stickers, plus marks, whatever—except candy or gum—I will. Cara understood that she had to work for me. I call it work because it is. A babysitter can play with a child. Often in college or graduate school, people pick up the attitude: 'Down's syndrome, well, we'll try to keep them happy, play some games, teach them a few words.' That's not an unusual attitude. But I believe you pump them full of everything you can. And the parents have to have a role. They have to follow through. If you have a speech and language pathologist who doesn't send work home, question it. There should always be homework assignments. You have to have long-term goals and daily goals and objective data to measure to see if you've achieved those goals. Parents ought to know those goals, too."

Patricia and her husband had recently moved to the Philadelphia area from Michigan State University where she had taught speech and language pathologists and had practiced herself. After initially testing Cara, she told us, "It blew my mind, if you'll pardon an unprofessional remark. She did so well on certain parts of the tests. In my fifteen years of work, I have never seen a Down's child do so well. I'm not saying there aren't children who can do as well, but I haven't seen them." Cara did particularly well, above her age level, on sound-blending. "I'd say a word very slowly with about a second between each syllable and then ask Cara to tell me the word, like 'tel' . . . 'e' . . . 'ph' . . . 'one.' And she said 'telephone' right away."

At first Patricia thought this was quirky, but Cara continued to catch the right word. I said that I thought Cara did well on sound-blending not only because she had a good ear but also because "The Electric Company," which Cara frequently watches, features a sound-blending exercise in which two silhouetted profiles face each other; one says the first syllable and the other says the next and both then pronounce the whole word.

After working with Cara for some time, Patricia told me, "Cara has made me rethink a lot, because we have preconceived notions. The minute you hear 'Down's syndrome' you hear 'retarded.' But somehow, through the grace of God, I could get beyond those preconceptions and look at Cara as an individual."

Patricia knew that there was much more to working successfully with delayed children than getting them to speak clearly. She worked on problems like short-term auditory sequencing, for example, with which Cara initially had some difficulty. Patricia would say "dog" . . . "cat" and ask Cara to repeat what she had said. More often than not, Cara would say, "cat" . . . "dog." Patricia also worked on left-to-right sequencing, a prerequisite to reading and writing, by such exercises as showing Cara three picture cards in a line, turning them over, and testing whether Cara could remember them in the correct left-to-right order. This was not strictly within her job description, but Patricia is never shy about bending a rule if it will help a child.

Cara finished her first year at The Children's House in high gear. She was independent and comfortable in her class. She had the benefit not only of Patricia's one-to-one tutoring but also of the carryover into the classroom. Patricia's working in the school rather than seeing Cara at home meant that she and Ann Schwarz could keep in touch about Cara's work and Ann could reinforce in the larger classroom setting whatever Patricia had worked on with Cara alone. This give-and-take with the classroom teacher, Patricia believes, is essential to a delayed child's successful development.

One May day in 1978, near the end of Cara's first year at The Children's House, I was sifting through the mail. Cara asked for her mail. I handed her a piece of junk mail and went back to reading the non-junk. Then I heard Cara softly saying "ppppp" . . . "lllll" . . . as she pointed to the P and L of the word "plus." I listened and watched her more closely. "Ppppp" . . . "lllll" . . . "us" . . . "us" . . . "plll" . . . "us" . . . "plus"! She had actually sounded out a word! She had *read* a strange word. Not a familiar storybook word like "dog" or "cow" that she had seen a thousand times. A new word and she had read it!

I was so proud of her. She has so much potential stored up in that little head, I thought. I wonder if she sometimes does not tease me with how much more she knows than we usually realize. I was not going to let this opportunity slip. I grabbed a pencil and sheet of paper. I wrote simple three- and four-letter words—"top," "hop," "pop" (she already knew "stop" from stop signs)—and we began sounding out the words together as I wrote them. She often got the sounds right but could not carry them through the whole word. She seemed to enjoy it, but I did not want my enthusiasm for her new achievement to swamp her or confuse her with too many words, so I stopped after about ten minutes of writing and reading. But I decided to try this reading readiness activity in small doses almost every day.

Cara did not pull the ability to sound out "plus" from the air. She had been watching "Sesame Street" and, less often, "The Electric Company," for over two years. She had logged hundreds of hours absorbing phonetics from those educational television programs. That electronic experience had meshed with her school work. One of the earliest Montessori activities is tracing the shapes of sandpaper letters. As the child runs her finger over the shape of the letter, the child says the sound of the letter. The brain is therefore receiving not only the visual impression of the letter, but also its sound and the feel of its shape. Maria Montessori explained the activity this way: "As she traces each letter, she fixes its path in her muscular memory."

About the time Cara read "plus," she pulled another surprise. The Philadelphia Museum of Art sponsored a symposium on "Understanding Paintings." The segment of the program which interested me most was titled "Children's First Drawings" by Howard Gardner, a Harvard psychologist. Gardner discussed the successive stages of a child's first works of art and how the child's perception influences the drawing.* Gardner called the first stage, "Scribbling I": a young toddler bangs the paper and

---

*Since the symposium, Gardner has published *Artful Scribbles: The Significance of Children's Drawings* (New York: Basic Books, 1980).

gets a satisfying sensation from doing just that, banging. Then come dots, poking or banging the paper with a crayon or felt-tip pencil. Next are big scribbles and bearing down hard on the paper. In this stage, which goes roughly through eighteen months of age, there is no connection between what the child is doing and what she visually perceives, Gardner said. When the child turns two years old and enters "Scribbling II," the connection is made. Circles are closed. One circle may be drawn within another. Gardner called the third stage, "Romancing." It is a stage when the child talks about what she is drawing. In this transitional stage, when the drawing is not representational, the child may say the blob on the paper is a truck.

Next comes the "Tadpole" stage in which people resemble tadpoles. One large circle for the face, legs descending right from the bottom of the circle-face. At this stage, the child can tell you what she is doing and you could recognize it even if you weren't told. At three or four years of age, most children draw tadpole after tadpole. The preschool child cannot integrate all the parts of a drawing and misses big, important details, like the trunk of the body. The child at this age is good at single-object recognition, something Western picture books perpetuate, Gardner commented.

When they are five to seven, children enter what Gardner called "Artistic Flowering." They are adding more details to their drawings, and their imaginations seem unleashed. After age seven, a child's drawings become more conventional, more representational. This older child is trying to render spatial relations and wants to know the "how" of drawing.

Gardner's remarks and the children's drawings he used to illustrate his talk made me think about Cara's drawings and David's as well. David, just over two, had already embarked on a scribbling career. Children like David pick up a crayon and move from scribbling through tadpoles to representational drawing with ease, some with considerable talent, others with less. A child like Cara does not often move through these stages so gracefully, and Gardner's comments reminded me of how Cara's growth differs from that of a non-retarded child. When she was a baby, Mattie worked with Cara on holding a fat pencil and drawing circles by moving her arm in big strokes. The purpose was not to teach Cara to draw a perfect circle, but to develop her motor control—fine motor with the pencil, gross motor with the wide arc of her arm. Cara's artwork was not meant to create a little Mary Cassatt but to develop her physical-mental coordination.

A few days before I heard Howard Gardner, I had noticed that Cara showed an interest in controlling her paintbrush. She painted closed circles and circles on top of other circles in one continuous stroke. She seemed to be trying to control the instrument in her hand instead of simply scribbling. Gardner's talk made me realize that Cara was progressing along the same lines all children do. She, too, had done a lot of Seurat-style dots before scribbling circles. But her art development, aside from exercises for specific developmental purposes, had been freewheeling up to that point. After hearing Gardner, I began to think that it would not do any harm, and might do some good, to structure her drawing and painting gently without stifling her creativity or pleasure. Gardner had also said that children can be pushed into drawing more mature figures at earlier ages, but he did not advocate this. We had been gently pushing Cara for four years; why not a little artistic push?

One rainy afternoon I pulled out a fresh batch of paper and clamped it on Cara's easel, which stood in a corner of the kitchen. "Let's draw a face," I suggested. She showed no interest in drawing it herself, so I drew a circle, two smaller circles for eyes, a tiny circle for a nose and a curved line for a mouth.

"Who's that?" Cara asked.

"I don't know. Who do you want it to be?" I asked.

"I don't know. Maybe Mimi." Mimi was one of David's teachers in the two-morning-a-week toddler class he attended.

"Okay, now it's your turn to draw a face," I said.

"All right." Cara drew an almost-closed blue circle and stopped, uncertain of what to do next.

"That's good. What does a face need?" I asked. She did not respond, so I drew two circles for eyes. "Now what else does it need?"

"A nose." She scribbled a small oval between the eyes. "And a mouth." Under the nose she added a wide V-shaped line that extended to the edges of the face.

"Very good. Let's do another." I drew another circle.

"No, who's that?" she asked, pointing to the just completed portrait.

"I don't know. Who is it?"

"I think it's Bob," she decided. Bob was another of David's teachers at the toddler program he called "Mimi-Bob's."

Cara followed my lead, first filling in the details of a face inside a circle I had drawn, then drawing her own face-circle and adding eyes, nose, mouth and some zigzag lines for hair. After she had mastered that, she proceeded to do exactly what Gardner said three- and four-year-olds do—draw tadpole legs, two lines descending from the face. I could not believe it. Had she secretly slipped in to Gardner's lecture and listened?

From that day until she was seven, Cara showed little artistic imagination. Left on her own, she usually "scribble-scrabbled," as David disgustedly dubbed it when he was four. Her artistic style was to brush watercolors abstractly around a piece of paper until the paper was totally covered. It reminded me of Gardner's scribbling stage, when the child seems to get pleasure out of the sensory experience of playing with the brush or crayon and there is little connection between something perceived and the marks on the paper. Asked to draw a person, Cara would oblige, but she preferred the sensuousness of moving a pencil, crayon or paintbrush over a paper in a dreamy way. By the spring after she turned seven, Cara was beginning to use a more representational, controlled style. One day she brought home from school her first illustrated story: "I like spring. The birds eat worms." She had drawn above the printed words pictures of birds, worms, flowers and the sun.

Near the end of Cara's first year at The Children's House, Ann Schwarz told parents that she was pregnant and would not be returning to teach in the fall. Ann was a beloved teacher. She had been at the school for a number of years and some of the children in Cara's class were younger siblings of children Ann had taught. For a gift for Ann, the mothers hit upon the idea of making a baby quilt from squares contributed by each child in the class. Some of the five- and six-year-olds made their own squares with iron-on transfer drawings. But most of the squares were made by the mothers. Our contribution was a blue and white striped square with Cara's handprints in red gingham appliquéd on and her name stitched in a corner. On the last day of school that June, the mothers and children presented Ann with individual gifts. Cara handed her the last big box. Tears glistened in Ann's eyes as she opened and held up the brightly patterned quilt. And there were tears in mine. Ann had been a wonderful teacher and I only wished that she were returning for at least two more years of Cara's primary education. But I was getting acclimated to losing fine teachers, to believing that losing a good teacher was not a total disaster. There was always another good teacher who would somehow find her way to Cara.

Enter Kim Auch. The year before Cara attended The Children's House, Kim had been Ann Schwarz's assistant. During Cara's year with Ann, Kim had a small class of her own. The oldest of twelve children, Kim was right at home in a classroom of thirty. The children loved her. Kim worked at a day camp for preschoolers during the summer. I thought a camp experience would be good for carrying Cara through the summer and it would be an opportunity for Cara and Kim to get to know each other, before Kim took over Ann's class in the fall.

That July we vacationed at my parents' home and at a Rhode Island beach where Cara played social director, introducing shy David to nearly everyone on the beach. "This is my brother, David. He's two." When we returned in August, Cara and David attended Kim's camp three days a week. David would also be starting at The Children's House that fall, so I thought it would be a good experience for him to get used to going off with Cara, lunch boxes in tow.

Cara's first year with Kim was enhanced by Kim's assistant, Adrianne Slattery. Kim and Adrianne made a beautiful team. They were sensitive to the needs of all the children, but they had an additional dimension of sensitivity toward Cara because both had family members with Down's syndrome. Kim has a teenage cousin and Adrianne had an aunt with Down's syndrome. Kim once wrote, in a thank-you note to us for a wedding present, "My family felt very special toward you and toward our sweet special Cara. She is so beautiful and I feel so lucky to have her with me. I pray to God to give me the wisdom and special care our little one needs."

Adrianne's experience with Down's syndrome was a generation removed. She once told me how differently her aunt had been raised. "I'm always telling my mother how well Cara is doing," she said. "And I just wish my aunt could have had a chance to develop as beautifully as Cara. I can't help thinking how my mother's sister could have benefitted if she had been born in Cara's time and had the education Cara's had. But back then the attitude toward retarded people was to protect them and not expect much of them. My aunt had a nurse who always took care of her and did everything for her. The highlight of my aunt's day was to put a record on the turntable and watch it go round and round. That was the big thing in her life. Things were so different then."

Like Kim, Adrianne viewed Cara as a gift for whom she was thankful. In a thank-you note for a Christmas present, Adrianne wrote, "I pray you know how grateful I am and I thank you for Cara. She has brought so much more meaning to my vocation. I thank God for this special opportunity."

Kim and Adrianne could appreciate the extra significance of a milestone for a delayed child. My clearest memory of this appreciation is a November day in 1978, when I arrived to pick up the children from school. Adrianne ran over to the car. "I just wanted to be sure this got home safely," she said excitedly as she handed me a small stack of white papers stapled together. "Cara can *read* eleven words!" This was the first of many "booklets," as she called them, that Cara was to bring home that year. One word was neatly printed on each tiny page: "dad," "bug," "had," "ask," "soft," "pat," "him," "sad," "lid," "and," "bad."

A month later, in the midst of the usual what-to-give-everyone-on-the-Christmas-list chaos, I had the perfect gift idea for Mattie. We framed a picture of a smiling face that Cara had drawn, wrapped it, and took it to her house the Saturday morning before Christmas. While Cara and David ogled Mattie's silver tree, Mattie showed us a card from another Ken-Crest alumnus, Danny, who had printed his own name on his Christmas card to her. Danny had made great progress from the lethargic, remote days of his infancy four years before.

Mattie hugged and kissed Cara and told her how much she liked the picture Cara had drawn. It would go up on her office wall, she said. Then Paul asked Mattie if she had a pencil and paper. "We want to show you something, don't we, Cara?" he said. He printed some simple words—"cat," "was," "ask," "soft," and so on—and Cara read each one softly. Mattie was so proud of her.

"Oh, Cara! That's wonderful. Oh, Cara," Mattie said between tears and hugs.

I once had to fill out a standard pediatric form on Cara and David for the health maintenance organization (HMO) we had joined. Most of the questions concerned the child's medical history but one question surprised me: "What do you like most about your child?" The answer was easy for Cara. Her sweetness is what I have always liked most about her. She was a sweet baby, rarely fussy, smiling and cooing. As she acquired language to express it, her sweetness became even more apparent. When Paul came home at night, she ran enthusiastically to him, with her arms outstretched, saying with a voice of pure love, "Oh, Daddy. Daddy's home." There was no embarrassment, none of the self-consciousness that another four-year-old might show in the same circumstances. I sensed that Cara's pure, innocent outpouring of her feelings would continue for years. Her intelligence probably will not tell her that it is unsophisticated for a twelve-year-old to run and hug those she loves.

When she was at Ken-Crest, Cara comforted crying babies with pats and toys, and went through a period of crying in sympathy with another child who was crying. At four-and-a-half, Cara was walking home from a neighbor's when she saw two little boys fall off a bike. Cara walked over to them and asked, "Are you all right?"

As I watch her run to hug a grandparent or comfort another child, I sometimes wonder about the differences between the innocence of a child like Cara, whose intellectual level is below normal, and the guarded expressions of emotion that we "normal" people develop as we mature. I often wonder about the Adam and Eve myth. Would we all have been as innocent as Cara before the Fall? Does higher intelligence necessarily bring sophistication that reveals itself in indifference and uncaring, or in hurting others? Paul has often wondered, he says, whether there's a "normal" Cara still in there, veiled by Down's syndrome. "She would be a very bright, sensitive, sweet little lady. How much of her generosity is simplicity?" he wonders.

When I fall into that thought pattern of what-if-she-didn't-have-Down's-syndrome, I always snap back to reality by thinking, "What difference does it make, anyway? She is who she is. Why waste time wondering?"

As Cara has grown older, she has not lost her innate sweetness but she has grown a bit tougher. At age eight, she often willingly shares things with David. But when he asks her for something that she does not wish to

share, she firmly stands her ground. If he provokes her, she argues with him and, if he takes what she does not want to surrender, she comes running to squeal on him. I am glad to see her stand up for herself, but I urge her to work out a solution with David rather than tattling. I realize, with a weary smile, that my sweet daughter is growing up. Tattling is a normal stage and Cara is passing through it.

If I had to analyze Cara's sweetness, I would say that 90 percent of it is innate and 10 percent is learned. One Saturday when Cara was about four, some friends dropped by. When they were leaving, Cara volunteered, "Thank you for coming, Jerry and Lois." They were surprised and touched by her expression. So was Paul. "Did you hear what she said? Isn't she the sweetest thing?" he later asked me. I agreed but I did not want to dampen his delight by adding that I had also said, "Thank you for coming," only a few minutes before Cara. Cara was not simply mimicking me. She was genuinely grateful for Jerry and Lois' visit. She had fallen all over Lois and at one point interrupted me with, "Stop talking, Mommy, I want to talk to Lois." Cara's sharp ears had picked up what I had said and she repeated my words later at an appropriate moment. Her feelings were real and she had learned the words to express them.

Just as Cara's sweetness blossomed with her growing use of language, so did her independent streak. A few weeks after she turned five, we were only four miles into a 220-mile trip to my parents' home when we had car trouble. We limped into a gas station but the surly station manager said he could not look at the car for another few hours. Paul would stay with the car but I had no intention of amusing two children at a garage for several hours. I called a taxi. When it arrived, we unloaded all our suitcases and kid paraphernalia and stuffed them into the taxi to return home. As we loaded the cab, Cara protested indignantly, "No, wait! This is all mixed up. I want to go to Gabby's" (Gabby is her name for my mother). She was annoyed until I pacified her with the picnic lunch we had planned to have on the trip. We broke open the lunch on our front sidewalk instead. After the car was repaired and we arrived at my parents' five hours later, Cara told Gabby immediately about how "everything was all mixed up and we had to take a taxi home." She has often recalled the incident and I assume it has great significance for her.

Most preschool-age children are total motion. Cara's physical movements are less graceful and coordinated than most children's and her
physical pace is often slower. Yet she is hardly a spectator. Cara bursts
onto a playground the way a ravenous guest attacks a lavish buffet. She
proceeds from one piece of play equipment to the next, samples each
one and misses none. First the climbing equipment, then the swings
(where she sings, "swing so high, swing a swing; everybody swing a
swing with me," her version of some "Sesame Street" song), and on to the
tunnel and the balance beam, until she has completed the full circuit. She
will then return to a particular favorite for a second helping. If a piece of
playground equipment is too high to reach or too difficult in some way,
she tries her best to conquer it.

When David was three and Cara five, David was far more cautious than
his big sister. While Cara attacked a playground by trying everything, David surveyed the whole scene with his eyes and only tried things he
judged safe. As I watched their different playground styles, I realized that
their intellectual differences lead each of them to different learning styles
even on a playground. Cara learns by doing, by trying something new
without any forethought. David looks at a scene and imagines what
would happen if he were to climb a ladder to a sliding board. He can tell
by looking if the steps are too high for him. Yet David is no scaredycat.
When he was only three, he shocked me with a calm "Hi, Mommy" from
twenty feet up a spiral stair inside a playground rocketship, then climbed
down as confidently and surefootedly as he had climbed up.

The Children's House has a movement-coordination program for
three- to six-year-olds called kindergym. Diane Vreugdenhil, a Montessori teacher and U.S. Olympic oarswoman, ran the kindergym during Cara
and David's primary years. Depending on the child's age and skill level,
the children explored their relationship to the physical space around
them by walking on a balance beam, jumping over a rope that was raised
higher each time, jumping on a trampoline, or climbing through geo-
metrically shaped frames. Behind the fun, some substantial steps in mental as well as physical development were taking place. As Dr. Montessori
said, "Mental development must be connected with movement and be
dependent on it."

One developmental step builds upon an earlier one: a child's readiness to read and write depends on many earlier physical experiences. Before a child can catch and throw a ball with any skill, he or she must be able to stop a rolled ball. Even that simple skill requires estimating the ball's arrival time and bringing the hands together at a precise moment—fingers, arms and eyes must work together. Once this is mastered a child learns to catch a large bouncing ball, then a somewhat smaller one thrown right at the hands, and eventually a baseball-size one. The eyes are range finders in these ball catching activities. When the child begins to read, the eyes must move across a page. This reading skill is enhanced by earlier successes in catching a rolled ball.

Diane explained the philosophy behind the kindergym program to a parent meeting the first year Cara attended The Children's House. She said that movement experiences are a vital part of every child's normal development, that all communication skills—reading, writing, speech, gestures—are motor-based abilities. Let children jump on the bed, somersault on the rug, try skates, teeter on a balance beam, because children who do not develop good coordination run a risk of perceptual and motor impairment.

For Cara and other retarded children, working on physical coordination is particularly important. In June 1978, Christine Rice, a PEACH physical and occupational therapist, wrote an eight-page "occupational therapy home program" for Cara. Many of her suggested activities were similar to those Diane used in kindergym, but it was helpful for us to have a written program to use over the summer. Like the skills developed in kindergym, those Ms. Rice suggested were sequential: first, stand on one foot for three seconds (this seemed interminably long and Cara had trouble standing that long for quite a while); then incorporate one-foot balance into games (doing the hokey-pokey, walking with one foot on the curb and the other on the ground); as her balance improves, begin hopping games (playing hopscotch, hopping in place to music, stepping in and out of boxes). One of the best features of our house is a forty-foot porch with a concrete floor. It provides plenty of space for hopscotch, low-key kickball and tricycle pedalling. Tricycle riding, I learned from Ms. Rice, involves "reciprocal movements," which simply means using two feet to alternate pushing in the same direction. This reciprocal

movement is the same kind of coordination that Cara mastered years before in crawling and walking. We climbed to still higher levels of sophistication in the reciprocal movement hierarchy: playing "Simon Says," we
would ask Cara to raise her right leg and left arm or to tap her feet alternately or to march to music while lifting her knees high.

I was aware of the importance of smooth reciprocal movement development because I had once written an article about children with perceptual or learning disabilities. For that article, I observed teachers being
trained to work with these children. To stress the importance of reciprocal movements' role in mental and perceptual development, the trainer
had some thirty teachers crawling around the floor on their hands and
knees. It was quite a sight, but it was an example of how teachers could
use crawling exercises, usually to music, to take children back to a developmental step they had not mastered as infants.

Ms. Rice's program was inspiring at the beginning of the summer. We
began these activities with a burst of enthusiasm but soon spent less and
less time on them. I have often regretted that I lost interest in encouraging Cara's physical activities. I think one reason that I slip in this area is
because Cara seems to be physically active enough on her own around
the house, at playgrounds, in the backyard on the swing set. As Cara approached age seven, she occasionally slipped back into the old pattern of
walking down stairs one step at a time instead of placing her left foot on
one step, then her right foot on the next. I realized then that we had been
neglecting physical coordination skills and immediately I began a "left-
right, left-right" sing-song whenever she walked downstairs. And I resolved to do more ball tossing, hopscotch and other games with Cara. But
like most resolutions, mine are never as fulfilled as I intend.

EIGHT

"She's Different"

In the fall of 1979, when Cara was five and a half, she took a giant step in her school world. She became an "all-dayer." For her first two years at The Children's House, she had attended five mornings a week. But the third primary year in a Montessori school is the equivalent of an all-day kindergarten for five- and six-year-olds. With becoming an all-dayer came the prestigious lunchbox, a clear sign to the "little kids" that you have become an upperclassman. Kim returned that fall but not Adrianne, who had decided to spend more time with her family. She was succeeded by Meg Roe who had previously assisted and taught art at The Children's House.

The first- and second-year children went home at noon or stayed in La Casa, the school's extended day program for children whose parents work. The five- and six-year-olds, however, had lunch, then went to work with Kim and Meg on reading, writing and math. In this way, the sixteen or so all-dayers received closer attention on what is usually called school readiness work.

At the beginning of this third year, Kim had a little talk with the other all-dayers about Cara. Kim was aware that these older children were beginning to recognize that Cara was different. "I just explained it to them in terms of differences," Kim later recalled. "I told them that Cara was sometimes slower to finish her work or to eat lunch. Slower to get ready to go outside. But some of us are slow and others are fast. Sometimes the faster ones will have to be patient and wait. Sometimes we help Cara but we want her to learn to do things for herself, too. And I talked about other differences, like I have dark hair and someone else has light hair;

you are tall and you are short; Gonzalo is from Venezuela and Allegra is Italian; and so on."

Though Kim pointed out these differences about Cara's being slower than others, she did not let Cara's pokiness inhibit the class. If the other children always had to wait for Cara to finish her lunch before they could go outside, they would grow resentful of her. Kim found a happy medium by asking them to accept Cara's differences and by encouraging Cara to keep up with the rest of the group.

In this third year at The Children's House, Cara's reading ability blossomed. She had her own primary phonics workbook that she completed over the second half of the year. This consisted of exercises in which several pictures appeared on a page with their names scrambled in a column on the side of the page. The child would have to take four similar words like "cap," "can," "cab" and "cat" and print each under the appropriate picture. Or there might be a scrambled sentence—"hen," "The," "is," "jet," "on," "the"—and a picture of a hen on a jet. The child would have to select the words in proper order and print "The hen is on the jet."

Cara had a good year with Kim and Meg but many of her skills were delayed enough, particularly in math and writing and her minimal conversation with other children, that Kim recommended that she spend another year as an all-dayer. Kim's recommendation did not surprise us at all. We recognized that a fourth primary year would be beneficial even though Cara would be the oldest, though not the largest in size, in the following fall's class.

Montessori children often talk about their class activities as "work." Cara, too, approached school as serious business. "I often imagine her striding in here carrying an attaché case," Patricia Bainbridge once remarked. Cara enjoyed her work so much that she often wanted to do it at home. In warm May sunlight, near the end of that third year, she was tracing words at our picnic table. After tracing each broken-line letter, she said, "I did it!" and I congratulated her. With solemnity worthy of an undertaker, she added, "It's very important." I thought that someone at school had pronounced this work "very important" and she was repeating an impressive phrase. A few moments later she came to me, hugged me and said, "Someday I go to high school. Then I'll be grown up."

Cara clearly understood why her work was "very important" and was not simply repeating a phrase as I had thought. I was touched by her aspirations but saddened. At that moment, I could not envision her in high school.

Another bright day the following month, I was reading a newspaper outside while David napped and Cara entertained herself in the sundappled yard. She had found a cup, a half-full bucket of rainwater, and a job to do. Repeatedly refilling the small cup from the bucket, she walked from plant to plant and kept up a running monologue about her work. As I watched her, I thought how happy she was in her own little world, being useful and independent at this task she found for herself. When she had finished, she came over to me and reported that she had given "all the plants a drink." She had given me a drink of great joy.

Cara's sober approach to schoolwork was fine, but it was also a root, I suspect, of her lack of socialization with her classmates. She answered when spoken to but did not initiate conversations often. Other children accepted Cara as another member of the class who was a bit slower and quieter. They were no kinder or crueler to her than to any other child. But she was not at the same "social maturity" level as her fellow five- and six-year-olds. She went about her business independently and alone—an attitude we helped foster from the beginning by saying, "You can do it yourself." I also suspect that she has a subtle realization that she is less glib than her garrulous classmates. She knows they speak faster, louder and more volubly. And her response is to listen, or tune out, or walk away. Cara is also somewhat shy, as I was at her age.

On the playground where most children socialize, Cara usually played alone on the climbing equipment. From the height of a jungle gym she once offered some observations to several children on the ground below. These usually loquacious children, accustomed to the quiet Cara, stared up dumbfounded, Kim recounted. They had not realized that Cara would volunteer more than a short, simple sentence.

Kim and Meg tried to structure situations within the classroom to encourage Cara to converse. Small group activities during the afternoon session would seem to provide an opportunity, but these failed more often than they succeeded. Once, after a speech session, Mrs. Bainbridge sent Cara back to the classroom with instructions to send in another boy for his turn. As Patricia watched from the doorway, she observed Cara go over to the boy and say quietly, "Billy, Mrs. Bainbridge." Billy was busy with something and either did not hear Cara or chose to ignore her. She repeated, somewhat louder, "Billy, Mrs. Bainbridge." Same response. Cara gave up on the boy and went to Kim to tell her that Billy was supposed to go to see Mrs. Bainbridge now.

Patricia related this incident to me because she was impressed with Cara's problem-solving ability. If Plan A doesn't work, try Plan B. Problem-solving is fine but the incident also illustrated that Cara's verbal authority was weak. Another child would probably have said in insistent tones something like, "Billy, I already told you. Mrs. Bainbridge is waiting for you and you better finish your work right now and go see her." Yet at home Cara could use her voice like a drill sergeant when her little brother got pesky: "David, I *told* you! That's *mine*."

During her fifth and sixth years Cara's ability to make connections and to express them creatively often amazed me. We once passed three television transmitters and Cara remarked, "Look, Mommy, a family of rocket ships." A few months later we received a card from a Southern California friend. Cara looked at the palm trees on the card and remarked, "Maybe Pom [of the 'Babar' stories] likes to climb on them." On the way home from school one November day, we saw an oddly shaped pine tree with three curved limbs branching from a short trunk.

"Look at that tree, Mommy."

"Yes, look how it's curved."

"No, it's a playful tree 'cause children can climb on it."

Cara was very aware of the world around her and her growing reading ability enhanced that awareness. She delighted in reading signs, magazine ads, and product names on television. Though I tried to limit the amount of time she and David logged in front of the television, she inevitably picked up certain jingles. Thanks to "Captain Kangaroo," "Nobody can do it like McDonald's can" became one of her hit tunes. She burst into song with this ditty as we entered a McDonald's for lunch one day when she was five, much to the amusement of the other people.

Cara also enjoyed reading cents-off coupons on the way to the grocery store: "Save forty cents [it was printed as "40¢"] on Sanka, the coffee that lets you be your best." I was impressed that any five-and-a-half-year-old, much less a retarded child, could read those unfamiliar words.

About this age Cara became a stickler for precision. "Take the cloth and wash your face," I suggested when she was in the bathtub. "*No*, not the cloth. The *wash* cloth. You know better than that, Mommy." Her penchant for precision sometimes became absurdly literal. When she completed a painting and said, "Oh, I forgot to put my name on it," I handed her a pen with the comment, "You can put your name in the corner." She took the pen and painting to a corner of the room and wrote her name—in the corner of the painting, of course.

We were driving home from school one day, a month before Cara turned six, when David noticed a house with an initial on its chimney. "Why does that house have an F?" he asked, and we got into a discussion of what initials were and what they meant. At supper time we again talked about initials and made up a guessing game. I gave someone's initials and Cara and David guessed whom I meant. As a hint, I gave them a context: "I am thinking of someone in Cara's class who has the initials R. F."

"Ruthie First," she said immediately.

"Great. Now I'm thinking of someone whose initials are G. P."

"Gwyn Prentice."

"That's right. Very good. I'm thinking about someone whose initials are M. B."

"Mia Blakeney."

"Terrific. What about J. C. F.?"

That stumped her. She could not come up with "John Christian Freeland." Even though he is always called John Christian, Cara could not make the leap from two initials to three. We then turned the game around and she gave me some initials to guess.

"I'm thinking of someone, N. P." I could not remember any child in her class with those initials. I gave up and asked her whom she meant.

"Gwyn Prentice," she said, perhaps choosing the last letter of Gwyn because it was the adjacent letter to Prentice. I corrected her and she gave me another pair of initials, M. H.

"Matthew Harker?" I asked.

"No, Mandy Hayden," she beamed. She had not only caught on, but had also thrown me a curve.

Cara asked me to do an alphabet puzzle with her soon after that. Each letter is printed on a separate wooden square and they all fit in a frame. I expected her to place the squares in the frame in A-to-Z order as she had done a hundred times before. As if to surprise me, she started with Z in the lower right corner of the frame and worked backwards. She clearly had the notion of reverse order, though she sometimes said "after" for "before." Occasionally she could not think in reverse to determine which letter preceded another, but she got most of them right. I was intrigued because she had deliberately restructured a familiar activity.

As Cara reached her sixth birthday, she became interested in writing. At school she had been tracing letters and printing them, but writing freehand was not easy for her. Her letters varied in size and wandered up and down slopes across the page. Yet she was not discouraged. She came to me one day and asked me how to spell "Maine." I told her, letter by letter, as she tried to print the word carefully in capital letters on a piece of yellow lined paper. She continued asking me spelling questions until she had filled the paper with "Maine," "Idaho," "Florida," "Canada" and "Spain."

Cara's interest in geography stemmed from puzzles at home and at school. The Christmas before she turned six, Cara received a cardboard puzzle map of the United States. Within a few weeks she knew the names and locations of all fifty states. After the evening news, our television occasionally stayed on long enough for "Tic Tac Dough" to appear. Cara loved this light-flashing, applauding, jumping-up-and-down game show. I tried to lure her away from it or turned it off, but I was amused one evening to walk into the living room and find Cara correctly answering a question which a contestant missed. The category was "maps of states." The game board showed a gray map of the United States with one central state illuminated in yellow. Asked which state it was, the contestant remained silent. "Kansas!" yelled Cara, correctly.

For her fourth year at The Children's House, Cara had another teacher. Kim resigned, and the children remaining in Kim's class merged with those in Maggie Brown Dougherty's smaller class, and Meg continued as assistant. Cara's reading continued to be her strongest area, but the fine motor skills required for writing and for math manipulations, such as moving and counting small disks or beads, were weak. Mathematical reasoning was still beyond Cara, so Maggie and Meg guided her in exercises that relied on her ability to memorize. It began with the simple table of adding by ones: one plus one, two plus one, three plus one, and so forth. By mid-year Cara knew it. In February she brought home a paper on which Maggie had written twelve equations in boxes such as 2 + 3 = , 2 + 2 = , 5 + 1 = , and 4 + 3 = . Cara had filled in the correct answers. This does not mean that if I asked Cara out of the blue, "What does 2 plus 4 equal?" she could come up with the answer in her head. Rather, she had found the correct answers on the sheet by using Montessori math apparatus to add concrete objects. This is the usual Montessori approach: children up to age six or seven learn through their senses from concrete experience and begin to abstract that knowledge later.

On the back of Cara's sheet of twelve equations, Cara had printed,

Cara Jablows Wrc is fatatc

She drew a smiling face and stuck a red star next to another self-congratulatory comment, "Gud Wrc." (Translation: "Cara Jablow's work is fantastic. . . . Good work.)

As she approached age seven, Cara began writing phonically and was so confident about it that she did not like to be corrected. When she was addressing Valentine cards to her classmates, she insisted that Stacy Mark should be spelled "Stase Mrc" and John Christian should be "Jon Cristn." After all, why bother with irrelevant vowels? I tried to correct her without dampening her enthusiasm for spelling and writing. When I said, "That's not the right way to spell it," she was indignant and went on doing it her way. So I tried another tack: "That's almost right. It does sound that way, but Douglas doesn't spell his name D-U-G-L-E-S." That approach was palatable. "Okay," she said, reaching for an eraser. Once again, Cara had taught me to find a more reasonable way.

We were having turkey for dinner one Sunday when Cara appointed herself waitress. With a clipboard and piece of paper, she took our orders:

> Pol Jablow   trce   win
> Matha   trce   win

| David | trce | milk |
| Cara | trce | milk |

I thought her phonetics were fascinating. C did have a hard *k* sound, particularly to one whose name is Cara, so "trce" does sound like "turkey." Cara had seen hundreds of "silent E" routines on "The Electric Company" but she had not assimilated them into her own spelling. Why shouldn't "wine" be spelled "win" then?

The most touching example of Cara's phonetic spelling came early one morning shortly after her seventh birthday. Often when she first wakes up, Cara is extremely talkative. She carries on monologues about getting dressed or chats with her favorite doll, Peter. On this particular morning, I heard her quiet sounds but rolled over for a few more minutes of sleep. When I got up, I realized that she had been into my good stationery. Before I could remind her "to leave my work alone," I found a sealed envelope with "Made Brusn" printed on it. Unabashedly violating Mattie Brunson's mail, I opened the envelope so that I could reseal it without Cara's knowledge. Inside was a carefully folded piece of my stationery on which Cara had printed, "Der Made Busen   I love you so I ned you." I soon found another phonetic missive, "Der Gal Tobe   I love you so I want you but irle* Tobe you and me." Cara had not seen Toby and Gail in nearly four years, though she has a picture of them in her room, and she had not seen Mattie in about a month. But Cara doesn't forget the VIPs in her life.

Her phonetic spelling fit Cara's pattern of taking things literally. In her style of learning, Cara leaves little room for exceptions or deviations. That is the way her mind works. Teachers, Paul and I have found that the way to work successfully with Cara—that is, to help her to be successful in whatever she is doing—is to build upon her inclination to be literal, to stick to the rules, to tread a narrow path, to take one small step at a time, and to repeat, repeat, repeat.

Christmas of 1980 brought an avalanche of puzzles to our house. Twenty-five-piece ones, hundred-piece ones, most of them with Snoopy themes. A favorite was one with "Peanuts" characters about to climb a

---

*She may have meant "early."

mountain with a banner, "Matterhorn or Bust." David was a puzzle whiz. He could complete a hundred-piece puzzle quickly by envisioning where a piece would fit even if the piece were sideways or upside-down. Cara was totally different. She would arbitrarily pick up a piece and try to fit it with any other piece. She did not become frustrated but we thought she soon would. Paul took this puzzle business upon himself as a way of teaching Cara to look for connections, to help her find some order in doing a puzzle that would lead to success.

Sunday mornings were my opportunity to sleep late. Paul got up with David and Cara, had breakfast with them, and tried to keep the noise level low enough so I could sleep. These mornings soon became puzzle-doing sessions. Paul broke down the big goal (completing a hundred-piece puzzle) into smaller goals (completing the sides) and then into even smaller goals (putting all the blue pieces with a straight edge together to form one edge). This was exactly the approach that has been successful with Cara since her earliest days at Ken-Crest. He suggested to Cara that she first find all the corner pieces, then the side pieces. "You have to look for the same color," he had to say repeatedly. He was the verbal coach; she found the pieces. After a few sessions, she began to pick up the concepts. Soon she was remembering that the "Schulz" signature was in the lower left corner and the copyright information was on four or five pieces in the lower right. She began picking out those pieces to start the puzzle. Paul knew she was catching on when, with only one piece missing in a particular section, she looked at the picture on the puzzle box cover, saw that the missing piece included part of Charlie Brown's scarf, and found the missing piece.

With a normal to bright child, a puzzle offers an opportunity for some mental gymnastics. The eye sends a picture to the brain of a jigsaw shape; the mind bounces that shape around and figures out how the shape, if turned a particular way, will mesh with other pieces. A child of normal to above average intelligence can make mental leaps from A to K to N to Z. But Cara's mental process moves one step at a time, A to B, B to C, C to D, and so on twenty-two more times to Z. Our generalized conclusion is that Cara can certainly learn, but learning is slower and requires repetitive step-by-step practice.

Since the day she left Ken-Crest, Cara had flourished among normal children. We expected this to continue until she was about twelve or thirteen, when we might find an educational setting where she could benefit from some vocational training. These expectations were based on conversations with a few parents and teachers of older children with Down's syndrome who had attended Montessori elementary schools.

Much of the literature about Down's syndrome contains information gathered from studies of institutionalized children rather than those reared at home. And the literature does not yet take into account the very recent advances made by retarded children like Cara who have had the benefits of an early intervention program. Therefore, when Paul and I read this literature, it was with considerable skepticism. We had seen Cara do far more than thought possible for a Down's syndrome child. Yet we did not cling to any hope that Cara would ever be "normal" in the sense that her reasoning power would become sufficient to allow her to live totally independently, for example, or to attend an academic college.

Our loose game plan for her future has been that she would attend Montessori elementary classes and later vocationally oriented junior and senior high schools where she would, no doubt, be in special education classes. But an unexpected question about our plan appeared in Cara's fourth year at The Children's House. When Maggie, Meg, Paul and I sat down for the first of the school's biannual parent-teacher conferences, we heard for the first time far more "can'ts" than "cans." Teacher conferences had been proud moments at which we had become used to hearing how well Cara was doing. Now Maggie was telling us that Cara's reading was good but her handwriting skills and math work, which require fine motor coordination as in counting out and moving small beads, were poor. Her socialization with the other children was almost non-existent. She often did not pay attention in a group activity. She was slow in completing work. Maggie knew that we wanted Cara to continue into Elementary but she raised the question of whether we had explored other options. She suggested that we take a look at other programs "as a frame of reference" and offered to visit them herself to see what might be best for Cara.

Maggie's candor caught me off guard. I was not expecting this sort of conference and my initial reaction was surprise. Maggie was not advising against Cara's going into Montessori elementary but she was concerned about whether Cara would be ready by the following September. She pointed out that the elementary school children do a great deal of work in groups and that Cara's reticence could hamper her. Maggie also feared that older children might not be patient with Cara's slow pace and might be cruel to her.

It was difficult for me to disagree. I liked Maggie a great deal. Even before she became Cara's teacher, Maggie and I had served together on the school's search committee to interview prospects for head of the school. We had shared rides to school and our children had played together. I respected Maggie's intelligence, her wit, her manner with children, and her ability to call a spade a spade. But Maggie is a red-headed Irishwoman and, though I do not have red hair, I do share some of her Irish qualities. I feared that we might dig in our stubborn Irish heels over Cara's future and I did not want that to happen. So, rather than telling Maggie immediately that I did not think her concerns were as serious as she did, I mulled over her comments.

Instinctively, I believed that Montessori was the right course for Cara. It had been working well for the past three years. Why shouldn't it continue? And I was not asking The Children's House to do something that no other Montessori school had done previously. Others had children with Down's syndrome and other handicaps in elementary classes with normal children. Nonetheless, why not explore other programs as Maggie suggested? It could do no harm. I began a flurry of phone calls.

First I called Patricia Bainbridge to set up testing sessions over the Christmas vacation. I wanted Patricia's professional—and sensible—evaluation of where Cara stood. Her results from two mornings' tests showed that Cara's school skills were on a par with average children in first grade.

I called two mothers of older children who had Down's syndrome and had attended Montessori elementary classes at another school. They reassured me that these classes had been beneficial to their children, that sometimes socialization came slowly but that wasn't a great hindrance to their children's success.

I also wrote to the director of a Montessori school in Cincinnati where exceptional children have comprised 10 percent of the school's enrollment since the school opened in 1968. I asked her how mainstreaming children with Down's syndrome had worked there. Sister Jacinta Shay responded that at her school, Mercy Montessori Center,

Our policy has been to treat the exceptional children the same as all the other children and to assess their progress each year. Decisions of number of years in each level rests with individual children. Most of the Downs have spent an additional year in each level. As the children grow older and more is expected in the skill areas, they are tutored one on one, or one to two by an auxiliary teacher provided by the State of Ohio. In addition, they receive tutorial speech and hearing therapy three times a week. Even though we have had some high functioning Downs, there have been areas, such as math, where they needed additional help and drill. Our greatest success has come in allowing the Downs the additional time they need to master the subject matter. They seem to be able to achieve in the same manner as the other children if they have sufficient time. We have been so pleased with our children and it is my ambition to hire them to work in our school in various capacities once they are old enough to be employed. At present, they are with us until age 15.

Perhaps your child's reticence to group activity is due in part to her not being at that social level, and/or that she doesn't have a companion with whom to identify. Our Downs children are in classes of 30 children, but their closest friends are the Downs children from the class.

I hope this letter is of some help. It is difficult to make generalizations about children unless you know them and their environments. God's blessings be yours.

I called a nearby school for exceptional children and made an appointment to visit. The school was so dismal, physically and educationally, that Paul and I concluded the visit with the admissions officer and fled as quickly as possible. We knew immediately that we would never spend several thousand dollars a year for Cara to vegetate in overheated classrooms with babysitter-teachers who send children to a cell-like isolation room whenever they become a teacher's problem.

I had once visited the special school for retarded children in our public school district with a group of Ken-Crest mothers. Housed in the oldest public school building in the city, it symbolized to me just where the School Board placed exceptional children on its list of priorities. I came away from that school with the feeling that I had visited a warehouse rather than a school. Cara would never set foot inside there, I had vowed. Yet I wondered what had happened in the years since my visit, with the implementation of the Education of All Handicapped Children Act (P.L. 94-142) of 1975. Though I had little hope for Cara in the bureaucratically snarled, nearly bankrupt, public school system, I reasoned that we were paying taxes for that system and we should at least look into it. One phone call set in motion a convoluted process of testing-teaming-labeling-and-placing (their terms, not mine) a special child.

The first stop was with a school psychologist who tested Cara. She and I arrived on the final, frigid day of December 1980 at the District Six office located in the center of a housing project. Urban planners had meant the school to be the heart of the project but it had become a magnet for the hostility of residents in the surrounding housing units. The high-rise buildings have been abandoned and the school building now houses administrators rather than students. As Cara and I waited in the stark, gray-green corridor, a janitor strolled down the hall with two administrators in three-piece suits. He was explaining how he had boarded up another broken window.

A slightly built man with a tweed hat on his gray head and a wool scarf around his neck appeared and introduced himself as Dr. Robert Rabinowitz. He led us into a former classroom now used for testing, set down his coat, hat, scarf and briefcase, and asked a few basic questions about Cara—date of birth, address (he noticed that we lived only a few blocks from him), and schools attended. I briefly filled him in on Ken-Crest, Bing and The Children's House. He asked a few questions about her development but when he asked, "What about her self-care habits?" I was momentarily baffled.

"Well, she can buckle her shoes, if that's what you mean. She can't tie shoelaces yet."

"A lot of first graders can't," he said. "How about her feeding? Can she feed herself?"

"Oh, yes. She's been doing that a long while," I answered. Wow, is he in for some surprises! He has the usual low expectations for a child with Down's syndrome. But let him find out for himself.

Dr. Rabinowitz said the tests would take about an hour. When I returned, Cara emerged from the room in Dr. Rabinowitz's arms. She had rarely been carried like that since she was a toddler. I knew instantly that she had become queen for the day. She pulled two small candies from her pockets and gave me a triumphant grin.

"She's won a lot of hearts around here this morning," Dr. Rabinowitz said, explaining that someone else in the office had given her the candy.

I assumed that the test results would be tallied and sent to us, but Dr. Rabinowitz asked, "Could we have a cup of coffee and talk? I explained that I had to get home fairly soon to relieve Paul from David-care so Paul could get to work by 2:00 P.M.

"Well, could I come to your home and talk with both of you?" he asked.

"Sure," I said, wondering why it seemed urgent to talk. As we were putting on our coats, a white-haired man passed and began chatting with Dr. Rabinowitz. I could not hear what they were saying but I sensed that it was about us. Suddenly the older man strode toward me, his hand extended, and introduced himself as Dr. So-and-So, Superintendent of Something.

"That's wonderful about your daughter. I'm so glad to hear how well she's doing. What a wonderful way to start off the new year," he gushed.

I did not know what was going on, but I said, "Thank you. Yes, she does very well. We think it's because she has gotten off to such a good, early start."

After the man left, Dr. Rabinowitz explained that he had been trying to convince this high-up official that the city school system should expand into early intervention programs. With Cara there as living, technicolor proof of early intervention's benefits, Dr. Rabinowitz had grabbed the opportunity to reinforce his point.

"Well, I'm glad I happened to say the right thing," I said.

Dr. Rabinowitz came back to our house and had coffee with Paul and me. He explained that he was quite baffled by Cara's testing. Clearly she had Down's syndrome, was retarded, was delayed in certain areas like fine motor skills, "but she doesn't test retarded."

He was impressed with Cara's test results as well as with her ability to interact with her environment. She is so verbal, he noted, "and so aware of her surroundings." His puzzlement told us more about his expectations for a child with Down's syndrome than it told us about Cara. He knew many, many retarded children, and many with Down's syndrome, but he had never seen one test higher than the retarded I.Q. range. And there was the problem.

The Education for All Handicapped Children Act (P.L. 94-142) mandates a "free and appropriate education for all handicapped children." It gives strong impetus to educating these children in the "least restrictive environment"—a key phrase—which means handicapped children can be placed in special or separate classes *only* when it is impossible to mainstream them satisfactorily in a regular class. The public schools could not place Cara in a special education class for educable mentally retarded (EMR) children, because it would be too "restrictive" for her, since she had tested above the EMR I.Q. range of 50 to 75.

As Dr. Rabinowitz talked, I felt I was experiencing another Catch-22. Cara had not qualified for the PEACH program because she tested too close to her chronological age. Now she was testing above range for a special education class. Yet she was definitely delayed by any realistic measure. Cara did not fit the bureaucracy's neat little pigeonholes.

Dr. Rabinowitz suggested that a placement in a class for learning disabled children might be a possibility. These classes were usually small, with a teacher and an aide for twelve children whose intelligence is normal to above average but who have specific learning problems. In an L.D. class, Cara would receive close individual attention in the areas where she was delayed. If we enrolled her in the public schools, Dr. Rabinowitz said, it would be wise to evaluate Cara's placement annually. She was close to normal now, he added, but later other children her age and grade would surpass her and the gap between them would widen. She might be in an L.D. class for a couple of years but later might be better placed in an EMR class. That sounded like the next chapter in the old "they-plateau-at-age-four-or-five" story we had heard and read when Cara was an infant. She and others who had been helped by early intervention programs and challenging preschool classes were disproving that myth. Maybe the gap would widen as Cara and her peers grew older. Certainly she is not as sophisticated an eight-year-old as most, but I bristle when anyone tells me what will probably happen in the future of a retarded child. Cara's future is unfinished. No one can predict it because her generation of children who have had early intervention programs have yet to create their futures.

With Cara testing above the EMR range, there also was the possibility of placing her in a regular first grade. I asked Dr. Rabinowitz about that. "That's possible, but she'd be in a class of probably thirty-five children whereas in an L.D. class, there would be about 12." Placement in an L.D. class was not Dr. Rabinowitz's decision to make alone. He explained that the next step in the process was an "educational evaluation" done by someone else. After waiting about two months to hear from the school system, we called them. Someone had failed to set up an appointment for Cara's next step, so we made the appointment on the phone. That test was the Brigance Diagnostic Inventory of Early Development. When Cara finished the test, the administrator, Karenann Moore, asked me if Cara had ever taken the test before. I said that I doubted it; I had never even heard of it.

"Well, she got many of the answers so quickly that it seemed almost as if she'd practiced on the test," Ms. Moore said. She added that Cara had done well in the reading and comprehension areas but her math was weak. Step number three was "teaming," which meant that Ms. Moore and another school psychologist who reviewed Dr. Rabinowitz's test evaluations sat down with Paul and me to discuss Cara's placement. They agreed on a learning disabled class, one in a school relatively near our home, a class where children would be close to Cara in age and who "would be very verbal, I'd hope," Ms. Moore said, "because she's so verbal."

Besides Montessori and public schools there was only one other possibility, a Catholic school for retarded children. But when we learned Cara's test results from Dr. Rabinowitz, we ruled out that school because it took only trainable and educable mentally retarded children. We saw no point in putting her in a class where everyone else functioned below her level.

We knew the Montessori school and what it offered; the public school environment was a total unknown. We could not visit a learning disabled class because the school system discouraged that sort of "shopping around." The system's line was, "Even if you did observe an L.D. class now, there's no guarantee that it would be the same class, teacher or school that your child would have next fall." We would have to wait until the school district made a placement for Cara. Then we could observe the class.

That March Maggie went on maternity leave. She had twin boys in April. Shortly before she left, we had another conference. Maggie and Meg stressed that they wanted Cara to be totally prepared for Elementary before she entered it. I appreciated their concern and told them so, but I also said that I was not sure any of us would ever be able to get Cara "totally ready" for anything. To keep her in primary another year, as Maggie suggested if no other options prevailed, would not challenge or help her, I felt, because she would be in a protective environment among younger children. I explained to Maggie and Meg that our approach with Cara from the very beginning of her life has been to push her gently but firmly, not protect and shelter her. I pointed out the experience of other children with Down's syndrome in the Elementary classes at the Mercy Montessori Center. But Maggie noted that there were small groups of children with Down's syndrome who socialized with themselves at Mercy, whereas Cara would be the only retarded child in The Children's House Elementary. Maggie worried that Cara wouldn't find adequate companionship. I worried less about that than Maggie, because I felt that Cara would find her own level of companionship in the mixed group of six- to twelve-year-olds. Outside school she seemed to play best with a child a few years older or younger rather than one her own age.

I thought, too, that Maggie and Meg were expecting Cara to acquire skills of average first graders without taking into account the fact that she does not develop the way a normal child does. It was something of a Catch-22 situation again—she came remarkably close to normal in so many ways that she was sometimes expected to be normal in all ways.

I think our conferences with Maggie and Meg are perfect examples of how parents and teachers can have honest differences of opinion about a child. They wanted to perfect Cara, protect her and prepare her until they felt she could hold her own in Elementary. I simply had a different approach, a riskier one, but one which I felt had been working for seven years: put Cara in a challenging situation and she will rise to it with some help. That spring we plunked down a non-refundable $100 deposit to enroll Cara in The Children's House Elementary the following fall. But I appreciated Maggie's making me rethink my plans and look into other possibilities.

When Maggie went on maternity leave, Adrianne Slattery returned for the remainder of the school year. Cara finished out the year happily, bringing home math work with proud grins. My favorite item from that period was a story that she wrote with the "moveable alphabet," a piece of Montessori apparatus consisting of individual letters, and then copied onto a piece of lined paper: "I like spring. The birds eat worms." She had illustrated it with birds, worms, a sun, trees and flowers. On the back of the paper, Adrianne had written, "Cara wrote this herself from the moveable alphabet. Hurrah!"

Soon after school closed that June, Adrianne told me that she was sorry the year ended when it did because Cara was just hitting her stride. She had even begun to participate in lunchtime conversations with the other children. I took Adrianne's observations as a harbinger of good things to come when Cara would enter Elementary the following fall.

That summer brought a change of pace, as every summer with young children does. The morning rush to meet the carpool gang was replaced by lazy breakfasts in our nightclothes. For several weeks, Cara and David attended a neighborhood day camp. There was no particular hurry to get there on time, as there had been during the school year. Cara and David enjoyed the arts and crafts aspect of day camp and Cara particularly loved the daily swimming sessions. They were grouped by grade with children who would be entering first through third grades. I thought this arrangement would be good for Cara because it placed her in exactly the same age range as the Montessori class in the fall. She managed quite well as their group took field trips and hikes in the woods where they waded in a stream to catch minnows in plastic cups. Her counselor later told me that Cara kept up well with the group even on long hikes on hot, humid days.

During non-camp days, we frequented a city pool where Cara and David could take swimming lessons. We made two trips to visit my family in Connecticut that summer. Cara made great aquatic progress in Uncle Bill's pool. She loved the water and came close to swimming the width of

the pool without stopping to touch bottom. When she discovered that she could do underwater somersaults, she did them continuously. I gasped when I first saw her do one after another without coming up for a breath.

By the end of the summer Cara and David were looking forward to school. We had received a list (pencils, ruler, folder, pencil sharpener, eraser, graph paper) from their teacher shortly before school reopened and we made a major shopping trip to Woolworths. Cara and David took this excursion as seriously as two adults shopping for a house.

For her first day in first grade, Cara sported a new lunchbox, bookbag, a pretty print dress and a white satin ribbon in her hair. As they went off to school together that first day of first grade, I knew my vision of them with their back-to-school clothes and their new school paraphernalia would be one of those snapshots forever fixed in my memory.

Cara and David were in a class of thirty-six first-, second- and third-graders. Their head teacher, Helena Grady, was assisted by Gerry Hartnett and Jonathan Levy. Their classroom had been renovated over the summer and was sparkling. David and Cara were both pleased to have desks of their own, which they did not have in their primary classes.

Throughout the early fall, Cara and David brought home bits and pieces of information about their day at school. Frequently one would start describing an incident and the other would add or correct details. More often, David, the faster talker, interrupted Cara or attempted to finish a sentence for her. This annoyed her greatly. "Stop that, David. I'm talking!" And it bothered me because I did not want him to develop a pattern of interrupting anyone, particularly Cara.

In November, Ms. Grady began homework assignments. Each child was given a monthly calendar with short assignments for every Monday through Thursday night. Two identical copies were taped to our re-frigerator door. Trying to be a conscientious mother, I wanted to make homework time a regular part of the evening routine. As I cleaned up the kitchen after dinner, I asked Cara and David to sit at the kitchen table to do their homework. Cara liked the routine. David fidgetted and hopped up to find something to play with instead. But he soon decided to com-pete a bit. "How many has Cara done? I'm beating Cara," he boasted as he rushed to complete his simple addition problems. His interruptions became so disruptive that I soon changed the routine and separated them. By mid-year, the homework scenario had taken on a definite style. If the assignment involved math, David breezed through it without being reminded to sit and finish. But Cara required my sitting next to her and helping her through the work, often with the help of an abacus. If the assignment was "read aloud for twenty minutes," Cara took off without any reminder and read aloud to a doll or herself, often for longer than twenty minutes. But David had to be prodded. I came to the conclusion that it is physically impossible for him to sit still for twenty minutes, just as it is physically impossible for him to walk when he can run.

If the assignment was to copy spelling words into a notebook, Cara readily did it. But as the year went on, and the spelling assignments developed into writing a sentence that contained the word, she often balked. "I don't know what to write," she would fuss. If I offered a clue, she would reject it with a whine and a squirm. The assignment initially frustrated her but once she had done a sentence or two, the other three came more easily and she would come up with some decent first-grade sentences such as "I like to feed the fish" for the spelling word "feed." She usually formed sentences with words she could spell. If she could not, she asked for help or accepted correction.

A parent-teacher conference in November was our first chance to sit down with Cara and David's teachers for a lengthy chat. The teachers showed us a stack of Cara's work—page after page of cursive letters showing vast improvement over the weeks, maps, math papers, spelling and language notebooks, a large picture of a tree with its various parts labelled. The sheer volume of work in less than three months astounded us. "You are really making her work," I remarked. "And that's terrific."

"Cara pushes herself, though," Gerry Hartnett said. "She has a lot more motivation than most first-graders."

As the teachers explained the work they were giving the children and the daily routine (children had to complete three items on their "starter list" before they could choose to do something else), Paul and I were impressed with the scope of the work and the individual attention each child seemed to receive. The teachers were pleased with Cara's progress.

They noted that she was not very social, but added that many children in first grade have not yet formed any strong friendships. We all agreed that Cara should be encouraged to participate in groups and there were many class projects which afforded such participation.

Helena and Gerry filled us in on David's work. "There's nothing wrong with his mind, but, oh, does he have a will!" Helena laughed. He would rather make up stories and illustrate them all day long than do anything else. "But he has to learn that he can't draw his way through life," Gerry added. They had discovered early in the school year that David needed firmness—he had to complete certain work before beginning his art work.

We asked how David and Cara related to each other in class. Helena said she had deliberately placed them in different groups for activities outside the classroom, French and music in particular. She also seated them at different clusters of desks in the classroom because such separation had worked well in the past with other sibling sets. But often David and Cara joined each other in a group activity and they talked to each other in the normal course of the day. Helena said Cara sometimes was a bit motherly toward David. At the end of the day, David's shirttail hangs out, his jacket falls off his shoulders, his mittens drop like dead flies, his bookbag flaps open, spilling its contents, as he rushes to meet the bus for home. The more meticulous Cara takes her time to get her things together. Helena told us that Cara occasionally picked up David's things or reminded him not to forget something. After one such time, she looked up at a teacher and said, "That David. He's so silly."

Another time, Helena related, she asked Cara to distribute some books to the class. When Cara came to David, she gave him the book and a kiss. "I bet he ducked under the desk at that," I laughed.

"No, he didn't seem to be embarrassed or to mind at all."

Cara is not always so loving with David. At home, in a moment of disgust with something David had done, she snapped, "David, you're retarded."

I was stunned, and somewhat amused that Cara was calling David "retarded" rather than the other way around. I had never heard either of them use the word before and I doubted Cara knew its meaning. I asked

her what retarded meant. "It means dumb." I asked her where she'd
heard the word used. She said a boy in school had told her she couldn't
do something because she was retarded.

I knew that Cara could never be protected from name-calling and I
knew that she was bright enough to know someday that she is retarded.
But I was unprepared for this first incident and it hurt. But, from the way
she relayed the incident to me, I didn't think she was hurt. She was accustomed to David and his friends calling each other "dumb-dumb," "poop-
stink," and other six-year-old epithets. To her, it seemed to be just another put-down name, one that had no personal meaning. But it hurt me.
It hurt that she was called a name, accurate though it was, a name that she
would undoubtedly be called many times in the future by insensitive
kids. And in the future, she would unquestionably be hurt by it.

I spoke with Helena about this. She did not know of the particular conversation Cara had told me about, but she did know that name-calling and
other insensitivities were fairly common among her six- to nine-year-
olds. She mentioned that a black child had been upset because he was
called black. "But I'm not black. I'm brown," he told his mother in distress. Another boy had been teased and called a girl—the worst thing a
little boy can be called—simply because he had curly hair. Helena told
me she had picked up on the latter incident as a jumping-off point for a
class discussion about what kindness is and how children can be nice to
each other. She asked me if I knew of any resources that could be used in
the classroom to prompt further discussion about differences and acceptance of them. "I don't want to pick just one example and focus on that,"
she said. "I'd like to deal with a variety on how we are all different."

I knew of some children's books about handicappd children and I borrowed some of them from the public library. I did not tell Cara and David
of my talk with Ms. Grady, but I showed them the books and told them
they were about different children some of whom were blind, retarded,
deaf or crippled. "Who would like to take these in to Ms. Grady?" I asked.

"I will," David insisted.

One of the joys of The Children's House, I have found, is that a parent
can feel totally welcomed in bringing a problem like this to a teacher. A
Montessori teacher is as concerned with imparting values like respect

and sensitivity as with imparting mathematical skills. From the earliest years, these values are part of the Montessori curriculum.

When Paul and I are asked about our expectations for Cara's future, we have no ready answers. We can look for hints over the past eight years and see that a spunky, independent, loving child is growing along her own unique path. She has distinct limitations. She cannot reason well; she has difficulty adding simple sums in her head. I cannot yet trust her to cross the street on her own. Though I have cautioned, "Look both ways and listen for cars," she still tosses her head perfunctorily from side to side in a quick, sloppy dramatization of looking in both directions. She does not look carefully.

Yet she continues to grow and to learn. Her questions are often intelligent. When I was reading "The Elves and the Shoemaker" to Cara and David one evening a few years ago, she interrupted me to inquire about two unfamiliar words: "What does 'gratitude' mean, Mommy?" "What does 'astonished' mean?" When I read the same book several nights later, I asked her what those words meant and she knew. Cara defies those who have maintained that children with Down's syndrome "plateau" at age four or five. She has such a solid eight-year foundation at the beginning of her life that I see no reason why she should lapse into other stereotypes about Down's syndrome.

I once found a so-called definition of mental retardation in a textbook. (I say "so-called" because Cara has taught me that there are no pat definitions.) It called mental retardation a condition "which renders the individual unable to compete in ordinary society because of impaired or incomplete mental development. Something, in other words, has happened structurally to the brain of the child, so that he is not able to learn, or learns more slowly than the average child. The mentally retarded child has poor judgment; his reasoning is weak; he has difficulty deciding how to act in new situations because he is unable to profit fully from past experience." *

As definitions go, that is not a bad one, but I would raise a question

---

* Edward L. French and J. Clifford Scott, *How You Can Help Your Retarded Child* (Philadelphia: J. B. Lippincott, 1967).

about part of it. Is it important to "compete" or to live with dignity and some independence within society? Cara won't climb any corporate ladders, but I can imagine her holding a non-competitive, dignified paying job such as assisting at a day care center or making floral arrangements at a flower shop, taking public transportation and perhaps shopping for herself.

I also wonder about the statement that a retarded person has difficulty deciding how to act in new situations because he is unable to profit fully from past experiences. How many of us are able to profit *fully* from past experiences? Cara learns something from past experiences and has not been stumped by how to act in a new situation. In fact, she relishes new situations.

I believe that Cara's future is unlimited when compared to the low expectations that have been held over the years about retarded people. Yet I am realistic enough to expect that Cara will not be able to live with complete independence. I would be perfectly happy to have Cara live with Paul and me for the rest of our lives, but there may come a day when she wants to fly the nest. Group homes are growing in acceptance as ways for retarded young people and adults to live in houses or apartments within a normal community setting. They are family-like groups where individual residents go out to jobs or classes and return each night. They take care of their own needs as best they can, from preparing meals to doing laundry, with houseparents available as counselors and supervisors rather than servants. Ken-Crest operates a number of such group homes, called "community living arrangements" by many agencies, and I can imagine Cara returning to Ken-Crest via this route in the distant future, if either she wanted to leave home or if we were too old, ill or unable to care for her at home. I do not expect David to grow up to become her custodian. Having a retarded sister will no doubt bring him moments of embarrassment and teasing. I hope that he will be enriched by the experience of having a handicapped sister but I believe that as an adult he should shoulder responsibility for her care only if he chooses to do so.

Those are such distant thoughts. At ages eight and six, Cara and David are good friends. They have their share of sibling arguments and tattling, but for the most part they play well together. David is often the instigator of their play and Cara his usually willing accomplice. So far David does not take advantage of her.

We are not certain how aware David is of Cara's handicap. He is not the kind of child, at age six at least, who will sit still for a heart-to-heart talk. If I tried to explain what retardation is and how it affects Cara, he would undoubtedly hop up and start playing. David has taught me that it is better to wait for him to ask questions than to give him explanations when he is not receptive. When Cara began reading a few years before David, he was quite aware that she had mastered a skill that he had not. He seemed to accept that simply because she was older than he. But when he began drawing masterpieces of detail around her "scribble-scrabble," as he dubbed her drawings, he realized that he could do something better than his older sister. When he questioned this, I explained that some people do certain things well and others do something else well regardless of age: Cara was a good reader; he was a good artist.

When Cara was nearly seven and David nearly five, Paul was helping Cara count to 100. She had been counting to 20 for years, but when she got to 29, 39 or 49, she could not make the jump to 30, 40 or 50. Maggie had explained that this jump is often difficult for preschool children. Paul worked with Cara by writing down the numbers in rows: 20 to 29, 30 to 39, and so on to 100. David observed this exercise and offered, "I'll teach her." He did not seem to comprehend why she needed a sheet of written numbers when he could count to 100 in his head, but he waited until Paul finished writing all the numbers before he started drilling Cara. Wearing his yellow plastic hard hat, David lay down on the kitchen floor with Cara and the sheet of numerals. Frequently interrupting her, he was not the best of teachers, but he tried. Later when Cara had left the kitchen, Paul praised David for helping her.

"Some people learn quickly and some people learn slowly. You learn quickly and Cara learns slowly. That means you can teach Cara even though she's older," Paul explained.

"Maybe when I get older I can be the teacher and Cara can be in the class. Sometimes a man can be a teacher," David replied.

In recounting this conversation to me later, Paul said, "That's the closest we've ever come to telling David that Cara is retarded. Probably I just did."

Once when I was reading an old favorite bedtime story, "The Very Hungry Caterpillar" by Eric Carle, I skipped the dedication page. Cara insisted that I go back to it, and she read, "To my sister, Christa." "What does that mean?" she asked.

"The man who wrote the book wrote it for his sister, Christa," I explained.

"Maybe some day David will write a book for me with lots of pages," she said.

Perhaps he will. Whether he does or not, their relationship over these first six years together has a solid base of love. On the morning of the day I finished writing this book, David came to our room very early and said that he wanted someone to go downstairs with him for breakfast. I mumbled that I was still sleepy and rolled over. A few moments later, Cara arrived and I suggested that she accompany David downstairs. She rubbed her eyes and agreed. Forty-five minutes later they bounded up the stairs to announce proudly that they had washed the dishes for me.

"I washed them and Cara dried them," David proclaimed. I imagined soap and water all over the counter and floor as I pulled myself out of bed. But when I walked into the kitchen, I found a neatly stacked pile of dry dishes on the counter, the container of soap considerably depleted, and very little water splashed about. As I congratulated them on their cooperation, I thought how sweet their companionship is.

Cara and David have far more differences than similarities but they are alike emotionally. Both are loving though Cara is more demonstrative with her affection. Both have easily bruised feelings but both rebound quickly.

Each brought me a flower within a few days of the other. David brought his into the house and handed it to me. Cara found a vase, filled it with water, inserted the flower, placed the vase on the table next to my side of our bed, and then came to tell me that she had a surprise for me.

Cara closes doors, shuts drawers, turns out lights when she leaves a room. David pulls clothes from a drawer and leaves it open. He only turns off a light when reminded. Running around with an untied shoelace does not bother him. I relish the differences of these two personalities and often wonder how two such varied children could possibly be siblings. They do not even look alike. Cara's straight brown hair and dark gray eyes contrast with David's blonde curls and light blue eyes. Cara's build is solid—it could become stocky if I do not watch her diet—and David barely has any flesh on his bones. He is a wiry dynamo of constant energy. Cara is more lethargic.

Apart from their physical differences, they are worlds away mentally. Where Cara is slow, David is quick. This often presents a problem in trying to dispense equal justice when a disciplinary problem arises. I try to avoid a double standard but it is sometimes difficult because some measures that will work for David will not work for Cara. He will push a demand or an action to its limit, and know exactly what he is doing, until I have to draw the line by removing him from the scene of the action or by withholding a privilege. But if I try that with Cara, it often backfires. If I say, "if you do that again, you will not be able to play outside after supper," she will reply, "I promise, I promise," with all the drama of a Sarah Bernhardt. Three minutes later she may repeat the same behavior. I am afraid that I am sometimes softer on Cara because her comprehension is less than David's. He is more demanding and I have far more confrontations with him than with Cara. Yet I tend to expect more of him.

Sometimes I catch myself wondering if I perhaps favor David. His sharp sense of humor, his clever, detailed six-year-old drawings, his ability to observe and absorb every detail of the world around him and ask bright questions delight and amaze me. Even when he wears me down with his insistent demands, I think of David's future as bright and unlimited. I suspect that he will make it in this world regardless of what we may or may not do as his parents. This is hardly how I see Cara's future. I certainly foresee hers as promising, but it will take much effort on our part and on the part of her teachers and society. She will make it, too, within her limits, but it will not be on her own.

When Cara was seven, some neighbors and I started a small tradition of having fatherless dinners together once a week. One father was working in Washington during the week, another was teaching an evening seminar, a third was beginning a new job in Miami and his family was to follow a few months later, and Paul was working typical newspaper night hours. We mothers decided to take turns cooking in order to share a meal in adult company. We ate in our dining rooms while the children ate in our kitchens. Among this group of eight children (the highest number before one family moved to Miami), Cara was the only girl in a crowd of boisterous boys.

Cara stayed on her own wavelength during these sessions as the boys shouted names at each other, bartered for each other's toys, or boasted of being bigger superheroes. She occasionally became the butt of their teasing—"That's a yucchy doll, Cara. Let's knock it off the chair." She sometimes came tattling to an adult but she usually maintained her cool. During one meal while some of the boys were clamoring for dessert, Cara placidly finished her pasta and sausage as the decibel level rose around her. When she finished, she quietly asked for dessert and cleared her place. The evening's hostess, the wife of husband teaching seminar, remarked, "My, Cara has such presence."

I was amused by her comment, but it was apt. Cara can concentrate on what she is doing and stay calm while all hell breaks loose. Some professionals in the field of mental retardation might say that Cara's "presence" is really just typical of retarded children, who are less involved in their surroundings, less aware, and therefore more placid. I prefer "presence."

These first eight years of Cara's life have been very good ones for us. She has been healthy; she has had an army of intelligent, loving, skilled teachers; she has been constantly challenged to take the next step on her developmental path; she has been loved by many people and has given love a thousandfold. All this good fortune has formed the bedrock of a life that, I am sure, will be productive, happy and as independent as possible.

Yet for all the advantages that Cara has had in these first crucial years, there is no guarantee that her future or ours will be free of worry. That thought was dramatized for me by an article in *The Exceptional Parent* magazine by a mother of a mildly retarded woman in her early twenties. The story related how successful the young woman's life had been in many ways. She held a job, could handle public transportation, enjoyed music and parties with her friends, and seemed determinedly independent. That was her problem, or her family's problem. She was so independent that she wanted a life of her own similar to those of other young women. She wanted an interesting job, a man in her life, an apartment of her own, and eventually children. Her mother related, in a direct and sen-

sitive way, the agonies of watching a retarded daughter break away from home. Though the daughter held a job, it was a boring one because her reading ability was nil and she could not advance beyond operating a duplicating machine all day. This frustrated the young woman, who was bright enough to recognize that she was boxed into a tedious, low-paying job. She wanted to earn more money to buy her own clothes and rent her own apartment. She left the family's home and moved into an apartment with a young man who was also mildly retarded and employed.

I suppose every parent suffers emotional shock at seeing a normal child grow up, leave home and move in with another young person. For this mother, the concern was compounded by her worry about the daughter's ability to manage her small income, to pay the rent and buy the groceries. Her greatest anxiety was the dilemma of the daughter's desire to have children. Were she and the young man capable of caring for a child? Did the mother have the right to interfere in their decision? The mother's article did not resolve these questions but it made me wonder what will happen to us ten or fifteen years from now. Will Cara succeed so well in becoming independent that we will be in a similar quandary? I would not be at all surprised. And I have no idea of how we would approach it. I can only hope that whatever decisions we must make about Cara's future will be based on her best interests, not our fears or apprehensions.

But Cara will undoubtedly give us direction in making future decisions as she has over her first eight years. As one of the first developmentally delayed babies in the country to participate in early intervention programs, Cara has truly been a pioneer. She and others who embarked on this adventure only a few years ago will continue to discover new ways of living in society and living with their own limitations.

NINE

"We Just Didn't Know

What to Expect"

In the preceding chapters I have told Cara's story in the best way I know as both a journalist and mother. Now it is my turn to make some statements of my own.

Cara has enriched my life with her outgoing, sweet, generous self. She has a spunky style that I find amusing and, occasionally, trying. She has proven, and I am sure will continue to prove, that low expectations about retarded people are outdated bunk. That is particularly satisfying to me as a parent.

Thanks to Cara, I have learned a great deal about attitudes toward retardation. The subject of retardation is uncomfortable for many people. Men in particular squirm and avoid eye contact when retardation is discussed. A tough newsman who has seen bodies blown to bits in Vietnam and has investigated sleazy politicians fidgets with the plastic swizzle stick in his Scotch when his wife asks me how Cara is doing. He tries to pay polite attention but his manner has changed from chatty ease to nervous silence. He is not atypical. Most people who do not know a retarded person well, or at all, pity the retarded and their families. The pity is well-intentioned but often misplaced or nourished in ignorance.

Retardation is simply a subject most people would rather avoid. In the first half of this century, most retarded persons were "put away" in institutions where the public did not have to look at their glazed eyes or drooling mouths. Enlightened people today know intellectually that moderately and mildly retarded people can function quite well within the community by living with their families or in group homes. But enlightenment in the head does not necessarily translate to enlightenment in the heart and gut. Emotionally, it is a different matter. Squirm, fidget, change the subject.

I understand this discomfort. I have felt it myself. While waiting for a train, I was approached by a young man who sat down next to me and began a conversation about his friend who worked in a pet store. The young man was clearly retarded, his speech understandable but repetitious. I would just as soon have been somewhere else. But I thought of Cara and hoped that a stranger at a train station would be a patient, cordial listener if she initiated a chat. I recognized in my first reaction to this young man the unease that causes many people to fear the retarded. And I wondered how much of that fear is at the root of many people's reticence to integrate the retarded into their communities and schools. A 1979 survey by the Gallup Poll and the Charles F. Kettering Foundation found that 77 percent of those interviewed believed that retarded children should be in special classes by themselves and only 13 percent favored mainstreaming them with normal children. Does this belief stem from a genuine concern to protect the retarded child from the real world or from fear and ignorance about how the retarded child's presence may affect the normal children in the class? Very few people understand or appreciate the two-way benefits of mainstreaming when it is handled by sensitive teachers: not only does the retarded child learn from normal role models, but the normal children learn by being exposed to children with differences. Perhaps the normal children will become more compassionate than their parents.

Until future generations become more accepting of their brothers and sisters with handicaps, uneasiness about the subject will continue. A frequent outlet for this unease is often an attempt at humor, which all too often turns into a sick joke. Once when day care agencies (and Ken-Crest was funded as one) were threatened with cutbacks from the state, Cara and I joined a protest march to the Pennsylvania State Office Building in Philadelphia. For her first protest march, one-year-old Cara slept in her stroller. As we marched up Broad Street past the *Inquirer*, Paul and his colleagues went to the windows to watch. One editor, not knowing Paul's child was among the protesters, shouted in jest, "Retardation Now!"

Several years later another colleague came to Paul with a Polish joke since Jablow is one of the few Poles on the paper. "What do you get when you cross a one-legged Polack with a mongoloid?" he asked. "A Polaroid One-Step."

While we note how insensitive people can be about the retarded, we sometimes joke about Cara's handicap. Perhaps we think we have more license when we keep it in the family. We were driving to a New Jersey pick-your-own blueberry farm one summer day when Cara started drumming a tune on something in the back seat. "I know what she'll be when she grows up," Paul said. "Cara Jablow, lead drummer of the history-making all-Down's band, the Downsbeats."

Experience is a major factor in an individual's attitude about mental retardation. The unfamiliar can be scary. When Cara was six months old, we vacationed at a South Carolina beach. On the way home, we stopped to visit friends who had not met Cara. She was dressed in a pretty pink smock and cooed happily in a bouncy canvas baby seat while we had brunch. Our friends were enchanted with this smiling, alert baby—and clearly surprised. "We just didn't know what to expect," Eva commented honestly. We have found that to be true over and over again. Friends and strangers are delightfully surprised to find Cara an engaging human being rather than the sluggish, bumbling moron so often envisioned when the word "retarded" is mentioned.

Attitudes about retarded people are not improved by most of the information available to the general public or to students planning to enter the fields of special education or medicine. One of the factors in the negative attitude toward people with Down's syndrome is the continuing use of the old name, "mongoloid." Even though Dr. J. Langdon Down observed and described the condition over a century ago, the term "Down's syndrome" has only recently gained acceptance. The substitution of "Down's syndrome" for "mongolism" erases not only the racial allusion to which many people of Asian background object, but it also removes the pejorative tone so long associated with "mongolian idiocy" and similar terms.

Unfortunately "mongolism" is still used by many who should know better. In *The New York Times Book Review* of May 25, 1980, the illustrious *Scientific American* used "mongolism" in an advertisement promoting an issue with an article on genetic defects. The ad said that "infants afflicted with 'mongolism' . . . are fated to lives of hopeless inadequacy and misery. No treatment exists for these or for most other abnormalities caused by genetic defects." Whoever wrote that ad obviously never met a child like Cara and never heard of early intervention programs.

On May 1, 1979, the Science section of *The New York Times* contained this statement: "All children affected with Down's syndrome are severely mentally retarded." Wrong. *The Times* did publish a correcting letter by Elizabeth Goodwin of the National Down Syndrome Society on June 19: "The fact is that the majority of Down's Syndrome children today are moderately retarded, many are turning out to be only mildly retarded, thanks to infant stimulation classes and a more positive and educated approach to such children. These children have suffered long enough from a public image that vastly underrated their potential." Hurrah for Ms. Goodwin's letter. I hope as many readers noticed it as read the original misstatement.

Some people collect stamps. Others collect beer cans. I collect horror statements about retardation. A sampling from my collection:

—"Mongoloids may also test high occasionally, receiving I.Q.'s in the 50's and 60's. Few if any of these should be considered as educable retarded since their other psychological and physical characteristics usually preclude their being able to apply their intelligence effectively in the achievement of eventual social and economic independence." That sorry statement is from a text published as recently as 1975 by Prentice-Hall. The book is *Education of Exceptional Children and Youth*, edited by William M. Cruickshank and G. Orville Johnson.

—"Frequently found in the trainable range of intelligence are mongoloid children—those with various recognizable physical characteristics resulting from a particular genetic disorder. (More recently, mongoloids are referred to as 'children with Down's syndrome,' since they then cannot be confused with the Mongoloid racial stock. However, the word 'mongoloid' is used for the sake of brevity.)" That gem is not from a 1920s textbook but from one published in 1974 by Columbia University Press, *Teaching the Mentally Retarded Child*, by Natalie Perry.

—"Pretty good for a mongoloid." That comment was made by a kindly white-haired pediatrician when he learned that Cara first walked alone at eighteen months of age. His comment rankled me but I later softened my attitude toward him when he told me that his grandchild had died of Tay-Sachs disease. "And when they did the genetic tests, we learned that it was my side of the family that carried these genes."

—Our 2,059-page, unabridged Random House Dictionary of the English Language (1969) was of little use when Paul looked up "Down's syndrome" shortly after Cara's birth. The term was not listed, though everything from "County Down" to "downwind" was spelled out in over two columns of "down" words. When Paul flipped to "mongolism" he read, "abnormal condition of a child born with a wide, flattened skull, narrow slanting eyes, and generally a mental deficiency. Also called Mongolian idiocy."

—"She assumes that I have all the acuteness of a mongoloid." Pulitzer Prize-winning novelist Wallace Stegner put those words into the mouth of his main character, Joe Allston, in *The Spectator Bird*.

—"Dear Abby, A friend of ours recently gave birth to an abnormal child (Mongoloid). We, her friends, are terribly upset about it, and the poor woman and her husband are in a deep depression. What should friends do under the circumstances? We certainly can't 'congratulate' the parents. Should we acknowledge the birth of this unfortunate child? Should we send a gift? (What does one send a Mongoloid child?) or would it be kinder to ignore the tragedy?—Bewildered

"Dear Bewildered, Perhaps 'congratulations' are not in order, but to ignore the birth of a child when you would normally express interest is, I think, cruel. So send a little gift (the same as you would to any other child) and show a continuing interest (not curiosity)." This "Dear Abby" column was headlined in 24-point type: "A Mongoloid Baby" in the March 16, 1977, *San Francisco Chronicle*. I agreed with Abby's advice to Bewildered, but I was sorry that anyone with her vast readership would let the term "Mongoloid" pass without correction. I wrote to Abby. She never answered or published my letter but she published one from an

Asian reader who objected to the term because of its implication that people of Mongol races have a mental deficiency.

—"Mickey the Mongoloid." That was a favored term applied to Mickey Mantle by a Yankee-hating New York Giants fan who had even less love for Dwight D. Eisenhower. He often called Ike "a mongoloid."

—In arguing that medicine should be rationed to control spiraling health costs, Harry Schwartz, writer-in-residence at the College of Physicians and Surgeons of Columbia University, suggested one form of rationing "might be a decision to deny free care to individuals for whom there is no good future, like Karen Quinlan." Mr. Schwartz added, "Expensive and heroic medical care might also be denied to those unfortunate babies born with Down's syndrome, or serious spina bifida or other ailments that doom a child from birth to a sadly reduced quality of life." (*Newsweek*, February 8, 1982, p. 13.)

For some parents, the shock of having a retarded child is so great that they need years, or take years, to accept the fact. Denial is natural at first: "It can't happen to me." But denial can become a quicksand. At some point, the parent must step out of the denial stage and move on to take an active part in raising the child as he or she is, limited to be sure, but still a human being with remarkable, unpredictable potential for growth.

One windy spring day, when the pale sun offered an excuse for getting outside, we took Cara and David to the Philadelphia Zoo. Four-year-old Cara ran from animal to animal without clinging to Paul or me. She was petting a sheep in the children's zoo section when we noticed another family whose little boy appeared to have Down's syndrome. An invisible radar system seems to exist in the Down's world—if there is a Down's child in the crowd, the parent of another will instantly spot him or her. We noticed the boy in a double stroller with his sister who was bigger and did not appear to have Down's syndrome. As we noticed the boy, his father saw us and came up to us. "Is that your daughter?" he asked, pointing toward Cara, "She's doing very well."

He explained that several times a year he and his wife brought their two-year-old son from their Midwest home to Philadelphia, where the whole family underwent a rigorous program to help the boy's development. We had heard of this program and, though it is only three miles from our home, had never bothered to look into it. Social workers and other professionals whom we trusted discounted this program as high-pressured and guilt-instilling if the child failed to come up to its standards. But we did not tell this father that. He sang the praises of the program and how it taught the family special exercises and programs to use with the boy. He did not tell us his occupation but I would have bet that he was a salesman and a successful one at that. We answered his questions about Cara and let him spiel on about his son's progress, which he attributed to this amazing program. He talked about how vigorous it was. "After all, we don't want him to turn into some kind of meatball," he said of his son.

While the man talked, his wife was curiously quiet. I thought I detected a resolute sadness in her eyes. My suspicion that this father had not yet fully accepted the fact that his son was retarded was confirmed when he said, "You know, I'm convinced that this program is so terrific that when our boy walks into kindergarten at age five with his twin sister, no one will know there is any difference between them."

We know another child with Down's syndrome whose mother came to accept her child's condition very slowly. There were two ironies in her story: the mother had amniocentesis and was told the child she was carrying would be normal; she is a specialist in special education.

Soon after the little girl was born, her mother found a doctor who would perform plastic surgery on the infant to make the "Down's look" around the eyes less noticeable. If that is not denial, consider this: the mother was directing a special education program at the time and used her daughter's picture on a brochure about the program. But she did not tell her staff that the child in the picture was hers. The mother also tried special vitamin supplements which, even its proponents concede, have not been proven to improve a Down's child's development, in the hope that the vitamins could help her child develop more normally. She enrolled her child in a regular nursery school. When Paul asked her how the teachers and other children were accepting her child, she replied, "Oh, no, they don't know she has Down's syndrome. I haven't told them. I want them to treat my child like any other child." When the child was about four years old, I ran into the mother after not seeing her for some time. She referred to having trouble accepting her daughter's condition.

That admission seemed to mark considerable progress away from denial toward reality.

Pearl Buck might have helped this woman with her description of how the author took a year off to spend as much time as possible teaching her daughter who had PKU (phenylketonuria). Ms. Buck wanted to find out what her daughter could learn. By the end of a year, she concluded that her daughter was able

to read simple sentences, that she was able, with much effort, to write her name, and that she loved songs and was able to sing simple ones. What she was able to achieve was of no significance in itself. I think she might have been able to proceed further, but one day, when, pressing her always very gently but still steadily and perhaps in my anxiety rather relentlessly, I happened to take her little right hand to guide it in writing a word. It was wet with perspiration. I took both her hands and opened them and saw they were wet. I realized then that the child was under intense strain, that she was trying her very best for my sake, submitting to something she did not in the least understand, with an angelic wish to please me. She was not really learning anything.

It seemed my heart broke all over again. When I could control myself I got up and put away the books forever. Of what use was it to push this mind beyond where it could function? She might after much effort be able to read a little, but she could never enjoy books. She might learn to write her name, but she would never find in writing a means of communication. Music she could hear with joy, but she could not make it. Yet the child was human. She had a right to happiness, and her happiness was to be able to live where she could function.*

I would probably not have put the books away forever, but I agree with Pearl Buck that a retarded child has a right to happiness and that happiness is dependent on living where the child can function. Our special

* *The Child Who Never Grew* (New York: The John Day Co., 1950), pp. 38–39. At the time Pearl Buck wrote the book, she did not know the specific diagnosis of PKU. Dramatic breakthroughs in the treatment of PKU were made in the 1950s and 1960s. Today routine tests are performed on newborns to detect PKU. If it is found, dietary treatment can now control it and prevent mental retardation.

children need help to function as best they can. They need stimulation and challenge and reinforcement. Perhaps they need our acceptance most of all.

There is a Chinese tale which speaks to this. A woman whose child died could not accept the death. She went to a Buddha who gave her a mustard seed and told her to carry the seed around the village and ask at each house if there had not been a death in the family. She found all had. The Buddha told her to plant the mustard seed. "It will grow and die," he said. In this way the woman came to accept reality.

My acceptance of Cara's retardation was perhaps eased a bit by some rudimentary preparation. I knew little about retardation in general and nothing specific about Down's syndrome before she was born. Yet there were experiences winding through my life—something like the individually shaped and spaced stepping-stones of a Japanese garden path—that led to Cara. These experiences included knowing the retarded son of my eighth-grade teacher; a newspaper story I once wrote about a North Carolina family who brought their severely retarded son home from an institution where he was regressing; a *Baltimore Sun* printer's thanks for writing about handicapped children's right to education (his son was retarded); writing about the State of Maryland's attempts to mainstream delayed children in public school classes; an interview with Dr. Mary Ainsworth, who opened my eyes to the importance of a child's early years.

Such experiences, no matter how numerous, could never add up to equal, instant or automatic acceptance of the fact that a child is retarded. But they help in making the eventual acceptance easier.

In making acceptance possible, parent groups can be useful, because they give emotional support—"We have been there, too. We know how hard it is." These parent groups offer solid information about where to seek help for the child, how to lobby for better programs, or where to find a dentist who is willing to treat a retarded child.

But I have met some parents who get so involved with their causes that they neglect their spouses and their children, even the retarded one they set out to help. They do not take time for themselves. They do not have the time to see a movie or to get involved with other interests. Once we received literature from a parent group that was organizing a cruise for parents of retarded children. "Can you imagine being cooped up on a ship for a week with a bunch of parents all talking about their retarded kids?" Paul asked incredulously. "Never."

This is our personal attitude; I don't mean to judge other parents. Cara is a far lighter burden than other retarded children who have more serious problems. Other families have certainly had more difficult times than we have. And we all react differently to problems. But I would hope that many parents could find a happy medium between denying reality and becoming so engulfed by it that all family life centers on "retardation." For me, it boils down to a simple formula: you have a retarded child; you learn to live with the situation; you find help for your child and help for yourself when you need it; you go about your own lives as individuals and as a family. Many agencies for the retarded can arrange respite care for a retarded child so that the parents can get away for a weekend by themselves. Parents who take advantage of such opportunities can give up the martyr role—they deserve to—and be a little selfish.

A family's ability to accept and cope with a retarded child's condition could be aided by informed, sensitive professionals whom they meet as soon as the child's condition is recognized. Too often that is more the exception than the rule. We feel particularly fortunate to have found Ken-Crest as early as we did. But that was strictly good luck. I happened to see a magazine picture of developmentally delayed babies in an early intervention program. Our experience as reporters also prepared us to ask questions and pursue leads. For most parents, though, ferreting out information about where to turn for help is very difficult. Society has no mechanism for helping these families. Perhaps they will chance upon an understanding, informed nurse or pediatrician who can steer them to an infant program or another family who has a child with a similar problem. But more likely the family will be directed to a genetic counselor.

In talking with other families, we have learned, however, that a genetic counselor rarely offers the information a family needs immediately: "Your child has such-and-such handicapping condition. If you choose to raise that child within your family rather than in an institution, here are some possibilities you might explore, some programs you might want to look into, some families you can call who have a similar child at home."

A family will eventually want to know more about the genetic makeup of their child and what kinds of tests can be done to detect a recurrence of the abnormality in future children but that is not what most want to hear right away. Their immediate concern is for the infant in their arms. "What can I do best for this child? How will raising him or her affect our whole family? What can we expect his or her future to be?" Yet genetic counselors seem to be more comfortable with multi-colored charts and graphs and other impersonal data about tests and chromosomes.

I came upon a book by David Hendin and Joan Marks called *The Genetic Connection: How to Protect Your Family against Hereditary Disease* (William Morrow and Co., 1978) which disturbed me so much that I wrote to Ms. Marks:

I did not find any mention in your book about the positive side of raising a retarded child at home. You mention, on page 16 for instance, "the huge cost of institutional care of a child with genetic diseases— Who can estimate the cost of the anguish of a single genetically-caused miscarriage or the unnecessary and unwanted birth of a single child with Down syndrome or Tay Sachs disease?" If I might offer some polite criticism, I think it is unfortunate to link Down's syndrome and Tay-Sachs disease in that context because Tay Sachs is so much more dismal since it is inevitably fatal. A child with Down's syndrome is a joy.

I wish you and other genetic counselors would give another side of the story—we are finally moving away from institutional care. If genetic counselors would tell parents of a retarded child the great strides that are being made in infant stimulation programs which work closely with the child's family, more families would have a ray of hope to consider when they are faced with weighty decisions about their child's future. Raising the child at home, with the strong support of an infant stimulation program, is the way to go for the future. It is best for the child and it is invaluable for the parents. It gives them emotional as well as informational support and it eliminates the guilt of parents who institutionalize their children. I think the positive sides of raising a brain-damaged or retarded child should be pointed out to parents both at the time of amniocentesis and immediately after the birth of a handicapped child. Parents need all the information they can get at these crucial times and I feel it is just as important for them to know this side as to know the genetic map of their child or the cost of institutionalization.

Ms. Marks replied to my letter:

Perhaps you are right that David Hendin and I did not deal with the positive aspects of raising a child with an inherited condition. Our emphasis, however, was on preventing genetic disease before it is transmitted. Since we would both agree with you that parents need all the information they can get, I think you have made an important suggestion that can, perhaps, be incorporated in subsequent printings.

What genetic counselors are striving for today is to present to parents, in an unbiased way, information which will enable them to make the decision that is right for them, rather than to burden them with counseling that places a moral responsibility to act one way or another. I hope that in your book you, too, will be able to avoid decision-making for others. Your own experiences should be demonstration enough of the benefits of the choice you have made.

Ms. Marks is right. I certainly want to avoid decision-making for others. My point, however, is that before parents can make their own decisions, they need practical information. Information about raising a retarded child at home or enrolling a child in early intervention programs more frequently comes not from professionals like genetic counselors and pediatricians but from other parents.

In some areas there are "parent networks" which a parent may call to be referred to other parents of similarly affected children. These experienced parents can provide encouragement and solid information. Bunny Curry gave me advice about Ken-Crest, other programs, and Down's syndrome in general that was far more useful than that of any professional.

The mother of Steve, a Ken-Crest child, heard about the program from a relative, not from her son's pediatrician across the street from the Ken-Crest center. The pediatrician's lack of curiosity about the Ken-Crest sign and the children playing outside will remain an eternal mystery to me. No pediatrician, nurse, counselor or social worker told Mark's mother about early intervention programs when she was told that Mark had

Down's syndrome. She plowed through the phone book and called agency after agency until she tracked down Ken-Crest. Ken-Crest and other agencies hardly keep their services a secret; they try to make them known. Nancy Nowell, Ken-Crest's social worker, banged on medical school doors all over Philadelphia in the hope that med students could be briefed on improved services for the retarded, but she was constantly met with the attitude: "We know best; we are the physicians; there is nothing we can learn from a social worker." She had somewhat better receptions from nurses, but it was still a difficult task.

The medical profession still has a long way to go in accepting a retarded child as a full human being with the same rights as everyone else. We know a family whose son was born not only with Down's syndrome but also with a heart defect that sometimes accompanies Down's syndrome. The heart problem was a simple one to correct with surgery but if it were left uncorrected the child would probably not live to adulthood. If the same heart defect had occurred in a non-retarded child, there would be no question of whether or not to operate—of course, the surgery would be done. Yet the boy's parents encountered physicians who were unwilling to operate. They were saying, in effect, "Forget the surgery; let the child die in his teens."

The boy's parents searched until they found a doctor who would perform the surgery. It was done successfully and the boy is a happy, active child with a healthy future. Once more, parents were in the forefront of seeking help for retarded children and the medical folks dragged behind.

Probably the worst horror story I know about a professional's failure to help a retarded child is this one. The youngest of several children in a large blue-collar family was not sitting, crawling, babbling or walking at the same ages his older siblings had. His mother noticed these delays but they did not become a serious concern until the boy was about three years old. Throughout this time, the family's doctor had reassured her that the boy was all right, "just a little slow." She discussed the situation with her co-workers and neighbors who were also concerned about the boy. The mother, who had limited formal education, decided to find out for herself. She went to the public library. Her research at the library led the mother to believe that her son might have Down's syndrome. She confronted the trusted old family doctor, "Does he?"

"Well, I suspected so," the doctor said. "That's why I didn't give him the usual inoculations."

No, that is not a misprint. *Didn't give him the usual inoculations.* This physician deliberately withheld inoculations, even more vital to a child with Down's syndrome because of greater proclivity toward some infections than most children, because, we can only suppose, the doctor felt the boy's demise might be a blessing to the family.

The mother found a Ken-Crest center and enrolled her son. He managed to make great strides there, though nearly four crucial years were lost thanks to this doctor. I asked the woman if her family still went to the same doctor. Yes, she said, he was nice and had been their doctor for years. I kept my opinion to myself but I thought, yes, I would have returned to him, too—but with a lawsuit and a letter to the Board of Medical Examiners asking that his license be revoked.

I can understand the poor judgment and negligence of an elderly physician who cut his teeth on words like "mongoloid" and all the myths that children of Cara's generation are beginning to disprove. But I am greatly disturbed by young physicians' ignorance and insensitivity. This new generation of physicians may be too sophisticated to use the word "mongolism" but many seem out of touch with developments outside their medical specialty. This was brought home to me by a conversation with a doctor who had attended the same college I did. Her first question about Cara was, "What are you going to do with her?" I was taken aback. Behind her words, I thought, was her real question, "Are you going to put her in an institution?" That was hardly what I naively expected from a young female doctor who shared my liberal arts background. But I concluded that her question was a logical one given her limited exposure to new advances for retarded children. She saw Down's syndrome as a pathology. She did not see a human child lovingly accepted by her family.

Physicians' training usually does not expose them to non-medical facets of child development. An early intervention program for a developmentally delayed infant is not a purely medical solution and many doctors fail to recognize its value. A prescription cannot be written for it, and it cannot be poured into a bottle and given in teaspoons four times a day.

Doctors are also trained to make firm diagnoses before they will suggest a treatment. Many children with developmental delays suffer from combinations of problems with nutritional, environmental, genetic or birth-related roots. Their problems may elude firm diagnoses. But if there is no label for the problem, the doctor may be reluctant to recommend a treatment. From this attitude comes the too-often-heard, "He'll grow out of it; he's just a bit slow." By the time the child clearly fails to develop along normal patterns—perhaps the child is four and not talking—the doctor has seen enough evidence of delay and finally makes a referral. But valuable years have been lost.

Early intervention programs are not much more than a decade old. There is very little evaluation of them in the medical literature. Couple that fact with physicians' unfamiliarity with non-medical treatment programs for very young children, and it is no wonder that traditionally cautious doctors are not yet in the forefront of those urging early diagnosis, referral and treatment for developmentally delayed children.

I do not condemn the entire medical profession for shortsightedness toward delayed children. Certainly there are many caring, enlightened pediatricians who support early intervention programs. But as a whole, doctors need to stretch beyond obvious medical diagnosis and enter into a partnership with parents, child development specialists, educators, physical therapists, social workers and others concerned with helping handicapped children.

Research is the one area where medicine is actively searching for help for the retarded. Certainly such research is important and may lead to valuable treatment or prevention of mental retardation. But I often worry that such "discoveries" or "breakthroughs," as they are reported in the media, unrealistically raise the hopes of parents whose children have a retarding condition. For them such research may come too late.

At Stanford University researchers have discovered that fetal cells show up in the mother's blood as early as the twelfth week of pregnancy. The significance of this is that a blood test could serve the same function as amniocentesis in analyzing the cast-off fetal cells, which reveal a great deal of information about the unborn child—its sex and genetic conditions, for example. Amniocentesis is currently performed no earlier than the fifteenth week of pregnancy and laboratory tests on the amniotic fluid take a few weeks more. A simple blood test performed on the pregnant woman would obviously be a simpler procedure than inserting a needle through her abdominal wall. The possibility of discovering a defect three or more weeks earlier in pregnancy is important because, if an abortion is performed, the risk is less the earlier it is done. The blood test is just the first step in this research, however. Dr. Leonard A. Herzenberg, who headed the Stanford team, said in 1979 that it would take years to develop a blood test that would reveal Down's syndrome in the fetus.

Another fairly recent medical discovery that may reduce the occurrence of Down's syndrome was proclaimed in 1978 with the unfortunate headline, "Hope for Future Mongoloid Victims." Once the reader got beyond the poor label, the news improved: scientists are zeroing in on the exact genes that cause Down's syndrome and, for the first time, are expressing hope that they may eventually learn how to reduce some of its effects. As we have known since 1959, Down's syndrome is caused by an accidental extra chromosome. But the recent discovery of Dr. Park S. Gerald of the Harvard Children's Hospital Medical Center reveals that only a small and barely detectable section of the extra chromosome actually produces Down's syndrome. Dr. Gerald estimates that the condition results from a limited number of genes which compose the chromosome, probably less than 10 to 20 percent of the total extra chromosome. If science can figure out which of these genes are causing Down's syndrome, they may be isolated and possibly inhibited.

Dr. Gerald's research is exciting for future generations but it is not expected to benefit those children already born with Down's syndrome. Woven into the good news about this research are some negatives. When Dr. Gerald reported his findings to a group of scientists and science writers at the annual Jackson Laboratory Short Course of Medical Genetics in Bar Harbor, Maine, in August 1978, science writers included in their stories statements like, "There is presently no treatment for Down's syndrome." Calling it a "disease," which infers it has a cure, referring to it as "mongolism," and failing to mention treatment like early intervention are serious errors by people who report on science to the general public.

Another story says that research indicates that retarded children's intelligence and general level of functioning can be improved if they are given a combination of vitamin and mineral supplements. It makes good reading and it offers hope to distraught parents, but the research study involved only sixteen children of different ages, sizes and conditions. I am not pumping Cara full of vitamins yet. I do see that she eats a balanced diet. If further research reveals that heavy doses of vitamins help, that will be wonderful. But I hope that parents and scientists will not seize on vitamins as the only means of salvation. Enriching a retarded child's entire environment at home and in school with the physical and mental exercises offered by early intervention and school-age programs can be more beneficial than any single solution.

Over the past eight years, I have been optimistic about the future for developmentally delayed children. Every day I have witnessed Cara's remarkable growth. When she was born in 1974, most accounts of retardation were bleak. If we had believed what we read then, Cara's future would have been forecast as one of childlike dependence on us and on society. If we had believed what we read then, we would have expected Cara to grow into a happy adult who probably could not read much more than her name and could not write or calculate enough to hold a job. We would have fallen into the trap of believing that she would "plateau" in intellectual growth about age four or five. If we had believed and expected that, perhaps she would have plateaued, because children usually live up to adult expectations. But we did not believe everything that we read. We took a chance on a new, unproven venture in the field of retardation, something called early intervention. We began to offer her challenges when she was only one month old. Those challenges took her from one small step to the next, toward independence and self-reliance. We do not expect Cara ever to be cured of Down's syndrome or to become completely "normal" but our expectations for her have soared far higher than they might have, had it not been for early intervention.

In May 1974, leaders in the fields of retardation, child development, education and pediatrics met at the University of North Carolina at Chapel Hill. Their conference, co-sponsored by the President's Committee on Mental Retardation and the Association for Childhood Education International, focused on early intervention. I knew nothing of the conference at the time—Cara was just nine weeks old—but when I read the conference proceedings two years later, I was heartened to learn that there were other people around the country who had established programs similar to Ken-Crest's. The research on screening, diagnosing and

teaching developmentally delayed infants and toddlers was beginning to spread.

The parallel between Cara's personal growth and the growth of early intervention programs since 1974 is striking. But I have recently become discouraged. Each year a funding crisis threatens the existence of infant programs. We have written letters to governors, secretaries of education and legislators. We have marched. We have visited the state legislature to talk with lawmakers face to face. My favorite example of these lobbying efforts is the flood of seven hundred letters supporting funding for early intervention that reached the governor's desk one year—many written by senior citizens who shared a building with one of Ken-Crest's infant programs.

Each year the state responded to the pressure of parents and friends of retarded children by allocating—at the last minute, with the last dime in the coffers—enough money to keep existing programs going. But there was never enough money to expand these badly needed services. Early intervention programs have battled on similar fronts across the country throughout the 1970s. Now, as children like Cara are proving the value of early intervention, its future is threatened more than ever.

When voters in the 1980 national election said, "Slow government spending and cut our taxes," warning signs went up for hundreds of social service programs. Four months after the inauguration, the Reagan administration announced its intention to repeal the Education for All Handicapped Children Act of 1975, P.L. 94-142. Even if P.L. 94-142 is saved from repeal, there may not be enough money appropriated to carry out its intent, since it has been funded at less than half the level originally intended when it was passed.

In these budget-cutting times, a right to education will be recognized only when it fits into a tight budget. A handicapped child's rights are only as good as the efforts exerted by parents and other advocates to ensure those rights. Unlike a multinational oil company or a military supplier, retarded children have little lobbying leverage among the decision-makers.

If federal funds for educational programs for the retarded are eliminated, parents and friends of the retarded will have to turn to their state legislators. Whether a parent is lobbying a Congressman or a state legislator, the argument to these budget-conscious, tax-cutting lawmakers can be the same. You can cut funds now and go back to the days when handicapped children sat at home until they were seven or older and were given silverware-sorting tasks year after year; or, you can recognize that early intervention programs could vastly improve their futures so that many could acquire productive skills and become independent citizens. The latter route will require more money up front, but if that route is not chosen the cost to society in the long run will be far greater.

Forget the humanistic arguments. Heartwarming scenes of retarded children feeding and dressing themselves at age four or reading at six will not win many votes in a legislature. More effective arguments are the economic facts. Try these:

—It has been calculated that it costs a quarter of a million dollars to provide a lifetime of institutional care to a retarded person. That is simply maintenance-level care.*

—The Department of Health, Education and Welfare (now Health and Human Services) estimated that mental retardation costs the nation between $6.5 and $9 billion annually in care, treatment and lost productivity. HEW alone spent over $1.7 billion on the mentally retarded in fiscal year 1976.

Would it not be wiser (translate "more economical" for the legislator) to invest in early intervention and public school programs for developmentally delayed children so that they may live more productively within their communities, rather than warehousing them in costly institutions?

In October 1977, the Controller General of the United States, Elmer Staats, issued a report to Congress titled, "Preventing Mental Retardation—More Can Be Done." The report was an outgrowth of President Nixon's stated goal of reducing by half the incidence of mental retardation by the end of this century. One of the report's major points was that there was no specific group within the federal bureaucracy designated with the task of reaching that goal. Among the report's statements were these:

—Mental retardation is one of the nation's greatest long-term public

---

*David Hendin and Joan Marks, *The Genetic Connection: How to Protect Your Family Against Hereditary Disease* (New York: William Morrow and Co., 1978).

health, social and economic problems. Although precise data on the extent of mental retardation in the United States are not available, authorities estimate that over six million people are mentally retarded and that over one hundred thousand new cases of retardation occur each year. Some estimate that as many as four million of the eighty million children expected to be born by the year 2000 (at present birth rates) will be or become retarded.

—About 75 percent of the incidence of mental retardation is attributed to environmental conditions during early childhood.

These statements could not provide better evidence for increasing support of early intervention programs. Yet the Controller General's report has been largely ignored. Over a year after the report was issued, I wrote to the HEW Secretary and asked what was being done to coordinate a national strategy to prevent and treat mental retardation, as the report had recommended. I never received an answer.

One of the first newspaper stories I ever wrote was one in 1965 about an early Head Start program. I have watched Head Start over the years as it was first lauded, then criticized as having short-lived effects, and finally accepted as truly beneficial. It probably will not be the last word, but as late as December 1979, a study by two Cornell University professors, Irving Lazar and Richard Darlington, concluded that Head Start does make a significant difference. They found that children in Head Start programs had higher I.Q. scores at age six and more self-esteem and better mathematical abilities in fourth grade than peers who did not attend preschool classes. Lazar and Darlington wrote, "We would ask the public and the policymakers to notice the strength of these findings and to reconsider their commitment to the nation's children, especially low-income children, by continuing to invest in preschool education. It is an investment in their future and in ours."

Just as Head Start seems to have established itself as a meaningful investment, early intervention for developmentally delayed children will, I hope, win wider acceptance. But that acceptance will only come with great effort. Recently I was talking to Dr. Barbara J. Marcelo Evans, a neurodevelopmental pediatrician whose children attended school with Cara and David. I told Barbara how Cara's test results had baffled the Philadelphia school system, because it could not fit Cara neatly into one of its pigeonholes. Barbara nodded and said that was one of the problems now emerging with children who have come from early intervention programs. "They come out of these programs functioning reasonably well. Their readiness skills warrant placement in a regular classroom or require only a small amount of time in a resource room. Their underlying disability is still functional and in a regular classroom the child quickly becomes overwhelmed by the lack of support." I was discouraged by Barbara's observation. The parallel to Head Start's history is unmistakable. Early help is terrific, but it must be followed up with appropriate, high-quality programs at elementary and secondary school levels. Otherwise, early intervention is simply setting a child up for a fall later.

If recent advances toward a brighter, more independent future for retarded children are to take root and grow, three basic things must happen:

—Policymakers must become aware of the need to assist retarded persons at the very beginning of their lives. Early intervention and school-age programs for developmentally delayed children must be funded at an increasing level.

—A full and responsible partnership must be forged among parents, doctors, educators, child development specialists, social workers, research scientists, physical and occupational therapists, lawmakers and bureaucrats and all concerned with helping the retarded to help themselves. The efforts of any one of these groups alone will never be enough to establish and maintain programs for the retarded.

—The public at large—those who are not related to and do not know a retarded person—must become enlightened about the rising potential and expectations of retarded people. Prejudicial words like "mongoloid" must be dropped. Examples of how retarded persons are living and working productively in their communities must become better known. Old myths and fears about retardation must be buried.

My hopes for Cara's future are simple. Twenty to thirty years from now, I hope that she will be leading a happy, full life, one as near normal as possible, that she will be able to hold a job that offers her satisfaction and dignity, that she will be able to walk into a bank, deposit her paycheck and budget her earnings, that she will share with friends and family a variety of interests. My hope for Cara's future is not so different from any parent's hope for a child: that she will be successful in living up to her potential.

I hope that Cara will be accepted by the community around her as a valued human being who happens to have certain intellectual limitations. I hope society will recognize that she has rights like everyone else and that she needs help from the rest of us in securing those rights. While I hold these hopes, I am not so naive as to think they will be fulfilled easily. Snags, insults, barriers will undoubtedly appear in her path. We will face and fight them when necessary. But Cara has had such a positive start in life that these first eight years cannot be negated in the future by society's shortsightedness.

EPILOGUE

A few months after Cara was born, in those days of grief that she had come into the world at a disadvantage, many people offered sympathy and kindness. One particular friend, Fred Kelly, added a suggestion to his expression of sympathy. "I know you probably don't want to think about this now, Martha, but maybe someday you'll want to write about this experience with Cara," he said. Fred's desk had been in back of mine at the *Baltimore Sun* and he had heard my typewriter clack out thousands of words on medical and education stories. I had always been the observer in those stories, never a participant. Cara has given me the opportunity to write a first-person story.

I have not written this as a cathartic exercise, though there may have been a few benefits of that nature, but because there is a need for her story to be told to parents and professionals alike. When parents first learn that their child is less than perfect, most have few places to turn. This vacuum only adds to their anguish. I hope that this book can offer them some comfort in knowing that they are not alone and that there is hope for their child. I am not suggesting that all developmentally delayed children will develop as Cara has simply if parents enroll them in early intervention programs or Montessori schools. Offered the same programs as Cara, some children may not function as well and some will do even better. Each child, delayed or not, is an individual who needs to be respected and cherished for those individual differences.

But I do suggest, by Cara's example, that all retarded children can develop to far greater degrees than previously expected if they are challenged and helped from the very start of their lives and if that early help is followed up throughout their school years. My hope is not only that parents of delayed children will hear this message and act upon it, but also that everyone concerned with the retarded will work to make this hope a reality.

LETTER TO PARENTS AND

PROFESSIONALS

The editors of this book have suggested that I add a brief letter of advice to summarize our experiences with Cara. I do not enjoy giving advice to anyone older than eight any more than I enjoy receiving it. But if it can help those who may return to this book from time to time, as their developmentally delayed child grows, I am willing to cite several points:

—First, families must grieve. The initial news that your child has a serious handicap is devastating. You have anticipated a beautiful, healthy, whole child for nine months of pregnancy and—wham—it is not so. Cry. Scream. Damn fate. But don't blame yourself. Then you will be able to get up and get on with life.

Professionals need to recognize and be sensitive to this initial period of grief. Families need the genetic and medical facts, but they also need sensitivity. As professionals present information to newly traumatized parents, they should avoid medical jargon; they should present the positive possibilities for delayed children; they should not rely on out-dated textbook knowledge. Professionals need to recognize the awe and power that they command from upset, bewildered parents. Their encouragement or discouragement can nudge a family in a direction they might not take in more stable moments. Therefore, professionals should not only give parents specific information about the nature of their child's handicap, but they also should make it their responsibility to direct the parent to seek appropriate help, such as local early intervention programs.

And long after the initial diagnosis, professionals should remember to support and encourage the parents' efforts with the delayed child. After a session with the child, the professional goes home and forgets the child until the next session. The parent can never do that. A few simple words of encouragement from the professional, perhaps about a small accomplishment the child is making, can keep the parents going as they live with the child daily.

—Second, parents who are not naturally patient must beg, borrow or steal a stash of patience. All children demand a parent's patience. A delayed child needs extra patience and time to learn, to walk downstairs, to button a coat. Offer patience, encourage the child to do tasks independently. Don't do for the child what he or she can do alone—if you do, you'll rob the child of pride and you'll foster dependency.

Parents and professionals will need patience with each other. They often look at the same child from 180 degrees apart. Both will need patience in understanding the other's viewpoint if the child is to benefit. And parents and professionals will need patience jointly in educating people who do not understand or tolerate handicapped people. But don't let your patience put you in a second-class seat. Parents particularly need to recognize when patience can lock them into a passive position. There will be many times when parents need to confront professionals or bureaucrats who have many years of experience and volumes of knowledge, but who cannot dictate what parents should do for their child. Parents need to weigh professional advice, and often seek second or third opinions, and then trust their own instincts in making decisions. Professionals, likewise, must respect the parents.

—Finally, parents and professionals will have to work as equal partners in helping handicapped children receive needed services. Society is not yet ready to offer all the medical, educational and psychological support that delayed children and their families require. Parents and professionals together will have to battle for handicapped children who cannot fight for their own rights. No one will come knocking on the door with a cornucopia of services for the child. Parents and professionals will have to demand them, and demand them repeatedly. This will have to be a coordinated, cooperative effort if it is to be effective.

I needn't add "love your child." You will, even through all the difficult moments. But I will add, let your child know your love and you will receive it back infinitely—just as Paul does every morning when Cara wakes him with, "Dad, your favorite is here."

RESOURCES

The following books, periodicals, films and organizations can be helpful to both parents and professionals who are interested in expanding their knowledge of developmentally delayed children and mental retardation. This list is not intended to be comprehensive, but rather a small beginning for discovering even more information. I have added personal observations about some of these resources.

Blanton, Elsie. *A Helpful Guide in the Training of a Mentally Retarded Child.* Richmond: Virginia State Department of Health. Available from the National Association for Retarded Citizens, P.O. Box 6109, 2709 Avenue E East, Arlington, TX 76011. This 33-page booklet contains rules for training, discipline, feeding, dressing and such.

Blodgett, Harriett. *Mentally Retarded Children: What Parents and Others Should Know.* Minneapolis: University of Minnesota Press, 1971. Sensible, straightforward and informative, this is one of the best books for parents and professionals. The author is experienced and conveys her practical knowledge clearly.

Canning, Claire D. *The Gift of Martha.* Boston: Down's Syndrome Research Developmental Clinic, Children's Hospital Medical Center. A short, sensitive softcover book written by a mother with photos by the father.

Caplan, Frank, ed. *The First Twelve Months of Life: Your Baby's Growth Month by Month.* New York: Grosset and Dunlap, 1973. Intended for parents of normal children, this book can also serve as a loose guide to parents of developmentally delayed infants because it reveals the sequential development that all babies go through.

Carlson, Bernice Wells, and David R. Ginglend. *Play Activities for the Retarded Child.* Nashville: Abingdon Press, 1961. Over two hundred pages of games, activities, and crafts that parents and teachers can use to help a developmentally delayed child grow and learn.

Chew, Mona. *The 1, 2, 3's of Teaching Color, Numbers, Reading, Language.* Beverly Hills: Ups for Down's Publications, 1977. The author is the mother of a child with Down's syndrome and a preschool teacher.

Gordon, Ira J. *Baby Learning through Baby Play (A Parent's Guide for the First Two Years).* New York: St. Martin's Press, 1970.

Hayden, Alice H., and Valentine Dmitriev. *Manual: Down's Syndrome Performance Inventory.* Seattle: Model Preschool Center for Handicapped Children, University of Washington, 1976–78. This inventory ranges from teaching prepositions to developing visual discrimination.

Horrobin, J. Margaret, and John E. Rynders. *To Give an Edge: A Guide for New Parents of Down's Syndrome (Mongoloid) Children.* Minneapolis: The Colwell Press, 1975.

Hunt, Nigel. *The World of Nigel Hunt: Diary of a Mongoloid Youth.* Garrett Publications, 1967.

Lane, Harland. *The Wild Boy of Aveyron.* Cambridge: Harvard University Press, 1976. The remarkable story of Jean-Marc Itard, the French doctor, and his accomplishments with Victor, the "wild boy" of central France nearly two hundred years ago; Itard's work gave rise to much of the educational treatment still used for the retarded. Novels, plays, poems, a film by François Truffaut and even a rock hit have been based on this story. Lane's book is a scholarly study.

Lévy, Dr. Janine. *The Baby Exercise Book.* New York: Pantheon, 1973. Great exercises for all babies that can be especially beneficial to those who are delayed.

Marzollo, Jean, Janice Lloyd, and Irene Trivas. *Learning Through Play.* New York: Harper/Colophon Books.

Montessori, Maria. *The Child in the Family.* New York: Avon Books, 1970. A good presentation of Montessori's observations about children, but I would suggest reading it after *The Secret of Childhood.*
————. *The Secret of Childhood.* New York: Ballantine Books, 1966. The best introduction to Montessori, in my opinion, for anyone interested in children.

Moore, Coralie B., and Kathryn Gorham Morton. *A Reader's Guide for Parents of Children with Mental, Physical or Emotional Disabilities.* Rockville, Md.: U.S. Public Health Service, Health Services Administration, Bureau of Community Health Services, 1976. (DHEW Publication No. (HSA) 77-5290.) A lengthy bibliography, well organized by such topics as legal rights, testing, speech, and speech handicaps, this book is an excellent reference for parents and professionals alike.

Newman, Irving, and Stephen Feldman, eds. *Readings in Down's Syndrome.* Special Learning Corp., 42 Boston Post Rd., Guilford, CT 06437. 1980.

Orem, R. C. *Montessori and the Special Child.* New York: Capricorn Books, 1970. This is informative for parents and teachers, whether Montessori-trained or not.

Prudden, Suzy. *Creative Fitness for Baby and Child.* New York: William Morrow, 1972.

Pueschel, Siegfried M., M.D., ed. *Down Syndrome, Growing and Learning.* Kansas City: Sheed Andrews and McMeel, 1978. In the series, Human Potential for Children. A brief but comprehensive look at issues, problems, resources and expectations about children with Down's syndrome.

Riesz, Elizabeth Dunkman. *First Years of a Down's Syndrome Child.* Seattle: Special Child Publications (Straub Printing and Publishing), 1978. This mother's record of her daughter's development over the first two years of her life mixes outline form and narrative. Contains many specific activities and records of achievement, and includes a checklist.

Roberts, Nancy. *David.* Atlanta: John Knox Press, 1968. A lovely, brief pictorial record of David Roberts' first four years. Photos by his father.

Shakesby, Paul S., and Peter Dorman. *Child's Work: A Learning Guide to Joyful Play.* Philadelphia: Running Press, 1974.

Shearer, David, and others. *Portage Guide to Early Education.* Portage, WI.: Cooperative Education Service #12. This is a packaged curriculum of developmental activities and checklists that parents can use at home and teachers can use in early intervention programs. Write: Cooperative Education Service Agency #12, 626 E. Slifer, Box 564, Portage, WI 53901.

Smith, David W., and Ann Asper Wilson. *The Child with Down's Syndrome (Mongolism): For Parents, Physicians and Persons Concerned with His Education and Care.* Philadelphia: W. B. Saunders, 1973.

This was the first book on Down's syndrome that we read after Cara's birth. The title promises more than the book delivers; it is far from comprehensive on education and care, but it does set forth clearly all the genetic information any parent would need. A section at the end contains parents' statements that are interesting and informative.

Spitalnik, Deborah, and Irving Rosenstein, eds. *All Children Grow and Learn.* Philadelphia: Temple University Developmental Disabilities Center, Ritter Annex, Temple University, Philadelphia, PA 19122. This 55-page booklet contains 21 activities that parents can use with de-layed children.

Tjossem, Theodore, ed. *Intervention Strategies for High Risk Infants and Young Children.* Baltimore: University Park Press, 1976. This large (over 700 pages) book contains reports presented at the 1974 conference sponsored by the President's Committee on Mental Retar-dation and the Association for Childhood Education International. It is virtually a bible for anyone who wants to establish an early inter-vention program.

White, Burton L. *The First Three Years of Life.* Englewood Cliffs: Pren-tice-Hall, 1975. Written for parents of normal children, this book em-phasizes the importance of the child's first three years, and thus the importance of early intervention for delayed children. All parents can learn from and enjoy it.

Periodicals and Organizations

American Alliance for Health, Physical Education and Recreation, 1201 16th St. NW, Washington, DC 20036, has publications of interest to parents and teachers of handicapped children. For example: "Physical Activities for the Mentally Retarded," "Practical Guide for Teaching the Mentally Retarded to Swim," "Early Intervention for Handicapped Children through Programs of Physical Education and Recreation," and "Get a Wiggle On," a booklet about helping blind or visually im-paired babies develop more fully.

Association for Retarded Citizens, 2501 Avenue J, Arlington, TX 76011, publishes a bimonthly newspaper, *The Arc*. State and local Associations for Retarded Citizens can also be very helpful through their publications and by steering parents to local services for their retarded children. If there is no ARC in your city or town, contact your state ARC (usually located in your state capital city).

The California State Department of Education has a series of eight brochures, titled "Parents Can Be Partners," that addresses questions about the Education for All Handicapped Act (PL 94-142) and parents' roles in procedures, planning, advocacy and mainstreaming. Write: California State Department of Education, Publication Sales, P.O. Box 271, Sacramento, CA 95802.

The Down's Syndrome Congress publishes *Down's Syndrome News* ten times each year. It can be obtained through Membership Services, P.O. Box 1527, Brownwood, TX 76801. The Down's Syndrome Congress's central office is located at 1640 W. Roosevelt Rd., Chicago, IL 60608.

The Exceptional Parent is a decade-old magazine published for parents of children with a wide range of exceptionalities. The address is The Exceptional Parent, 296 Boylston St., Boston, MA 02116.

The Joseph P. Kennedy Foundation, Suite 205, 1701 K Street NW, Washington, DC 20036, will send literature about various aspects of retardation upon request.

Sharing Our Caring is a magazine for parents of children with Down's syndrome. Write: P.O. Box 196, Milton, WA 98354.

Films and Videotape

Balloon People is a mime troupe's presentation of how retarded people feel and how they are seen by society. Its deliberately generalized and ambiguous staging is meant to generate group discussion. A ten-page discussion guide accompanies both the videotape and the 16mm film versions. Write: Developmental Disabilities Center, Temple University, Ritter Hall Annex, Philadelphia, PA 19122.

Best Boy, Ira Wohl's Academy-Award-winning documentary about his retarded cousin, who in his fifties broke away from the shelter of his aged parents' protection, is available from Documentary Films, Inc., 159 W. 53d St., N.Y., NY 10019.

Board and Care is a touching film about two young adults with Down's syndrome who develop a close relationship. This 27-minute color film was nominated for an Academy Award in 1980. It is available from Pyramid Films, Box 1048, Santa Monica, CA 90406.

Let Me Try is an animated film for children about a retarded child's attempts at independence. Write Encyclopedia Britannica Films, 425 W. Michigan Ave., Chicago, IL 60611.

For Children

Siblings and schoolmates can also gain a better understanding of retarded children through books written for them specifically. Here I list just a few; a children's librarian can recommend more.

Fassler, Joan. *One Little Girl.* New York: Human Sciences Press. Laurie is a slow child who learns to do some things quite well.

Klein, Gerda. *The Blue Rose.* Lawrence Hill, 1974. An allegory about a retarded child for elementary-age children.

Lasker, Joe. *He's My Brother.* Chicago: Albert Whitman and Co., 1974. Jamie has problems as a slow learner at home and at school.

Ominsky, Elaine. *Jon O. A Special Boy.* Englewood Cliffs: Prentice-Hall. Written for young children, this story explains how Jon, who has Down's syndrome, differs from and is like other children.

Quadrus and Friends. *A Friend in Need.* Philadelphia: Quadrus and Friends, Inc., a special project of the School District of Philadelphia, Division of Special Education, 1980. This is a comic book with two pages of workbook activities about accepting handicapped children.

Sobol, Harriet. *My Brother Steve Is Retarded.* New York: Macmillan, 1977. Eleven-year-old girl discusses her feelings about her retarded brother.

There are many children's books about physical handicaps that also help normal children understand exceptionalities. Bernard Wolf has written several: *Anna's Silent World*, *Connie's New Eyes*, and *Don't Feel Sorry for Paul*, all published by Lippincott. Joan Fassler's *Howie Helps Himself*, published by Whitman, is another. Ask local librarians for others.

INDEX